BIG LESSONS

❖

FROM A SMALL TOWN

BIG LESSONS

FROM A SMALL TOWN

By Bill Schuette

with Sarah Opperman

Arbutus Press

Traverse City, Michigan

Big Lessons from a Small Town © 2015 Bill Schuette

ISBN 978-1-933926-59-9 soft cover

ISBN 978-1-933926-61-2 hard cover

www.Biglessonsfromasmalltown.com

Arbutus Press, Traverse City, Michigan, editor@arbutuspress.com, www. Arbutuspress.com

Library of Congress Cataloging-in-Publication Data

Schuette, Bill.

  Big lessons from a small town / by Bill Schuette.

      pages cm

  Includes index.

  ISBN 978-1-933926-59-9

  1.   Schuette, Bill. 2.   Schuette, Bill--Philosophy. 3.   Legislators--United States--Biography. 4.   United States. Congress. House--Biography. 5. Politicians--Michigan--Biography. 6.   Political leadership--United States. 7. Conduct of life. 8. Schuette, Bill--Childhood and youth. 9. Midland (Mich.)--Biography. 10. Midland (Mich.)--Social life and customs. I. Title.

  E840.8.S365A3 2015

  328.73'092--dc23

  [B]

                                                      2015026969

Printed in Grand Rapids, Michigan, USA

Cover design by Autumn Gardner and Melissa Anderson - Quick Reliable Printing, Midland, Michigan

Author photograph: Kathy Morley, Morley Portraiture; Midland, Michigan

I dedicate this book to my wife Cynthia, who has been patient, kind, loving and supportive of me throughout our marriage and my journey in public service. Our children, Heidi and Bill, are amazing young adults, and reflect the love Cynthia has poured into them and our family.

Without Cynthia's love and steadfast commitment, I could not have learned and fully appreciated the lessons in this book, and it never would have been published.

Nobody said it would be easy and everybody was right.

— George H.W. Bush

CONTENTS

FOREWORD

Leadership is a developed trait. It is not inherited. It cannot be simply handed out to the next person in line. There has usually been a price to pay along the way. Sacrifice, experience, handling adversity, discipline, an attention to detail, success and general moral values all tend to define most individuals. It is along this path that leadership is earned. It is a lifelong journey that begins and ends with our life's experiences.

My path as a college football coach began over 35 years ago. It was preceded by a childhood filled with sports, a loving and supportive family and a solid education in a small Midwestern city. Like Bill Schuette's time in Midland, Michigan, my experiences began to shape me for a lifetime.

Coaches tend to have program philosophies. Ours at Michigan State University is quite simple, yet difficult to attain. Our basis starts with a relationship with every individual present in our organization. It must be formulated to last for a lifetime and must start at the ground level. It must involve a sincere COMMITMENT to every individual's life; the ability to COMMUNICATE and solve their problems both big and small. It must be built on TRUST. Bill Schuette has worked a lifetime in establishing this with his constituency.

Our second phase is based on EDUCATION and helping the individual become SELF-SUFFICIENT. There is nothing more gratifying than "Earning the Jersey" and standing on your own two feet as you move forward professionally. Check Bill Schuette.

The third component emphasizes WINNING; to compete and become the best in your realm of work or play. Bill again personifies this aspect of high achievement.

Finally, our fourth strategy is to be a GIVER, not a taker. To lead, you must first and forever be a servant. Bill has demonstrated this essential quality over and over.

Simply put, SUCCESS is about people. It is about finding the TRUTH in your endeavors and following it to the end. As I have grown to know Bill, he encompasses these qualities that have allowed our teams at Michigan State University to succeed at such a high level. He continues to REACH HIGHER as he pushes towards change and development in the State of Michigan and beyond. His book is an example of the above; a passion for people born from a life filled with both success and adversity; that of a leader.

Mark Dantonio
Head Football Coach
Michigan State University

PREFACE

We all have a hometown. For most of us, this is where we learned the values of community and service that have guided us throughout our lives. My hometown is Midland, Michigan.

This is a book about the most powerful life lessons and values that were instilled in me when I was young, and what I've learned along the way that might help you, too. It is also a reflection on what our small hometown communities still offer us today.

Values are big in small towns, and are considered a barometer of character. They include knowing the importance of family, honesty and hard work; looking a person in the eye, shaking hands and knowing your word is stronger than any contract; understanding the value of a dollar; and recognizing the significance of giving to and building your community. When I went to Washington, D.C., to serve in the U.S. House of Representatives, however, it was a challenge to remember those lessons and what service truly means. Looking back, I realize I was fortunate to have people keep me centered when I started to stray, and have since been reminded and come to better appreciate those life lessons and values. This realization was an epiphany of sorts, and has influenced me to capture the fundamental values that are rooted in our nation's small towns.

Small-town America, with its deep roots over many generations, has been hard-hit over the years, especially during tough economic times. A lot of small-town young adults have left home in search of opportunity elsewhere. A lot of businesses have also packed up and moved out of small communities and into large cities around the world. However, I think that if you're from Midland or a place like it, you'll find that hometown values are still very much alive, off every interstate, dotting the landscape across our country. Sure, they come under pressure occasionally, but they have survived the test of time and importantly, they still count – especially in today's fast-changing world.

It may sound hokey, but the towns I know are truly places where folks live in service to one another. People work together, play together and pray together. As countless community leaders—from volunteer firefighters to the boards of community centers—demonstrate daily, you don't have to be in elected office to make a difference. Often, the only—and best—compensation that local elected and non-elected officials receive is a stronger and safer community for their families and neighbors, and the personal reward of making a difference.

There are always those with means and those without, and small towns, like big cities, have their fair share of drama and turmoil. Middle America may include several towns named Utopia, but of course none actually are; nowhere is.

All the same, there's a closeness in places like Midland—a connectedness—that's hard to replicate in large urban areas.

It was because of that closeness and sense of service that I had the confidence to run for the U.S. Congress at age 29 to represent the community that had given me so much. As a young man just a few years out of college, and with the huge help of my family and so many friends, plus a strong dose of true "Midland mettle" (which we all have deep down inside), I was able to come from behind to unseat the incumbent congressman.

Once elected, the glitter and glamor of commuting to and from Midland to Washington, D.C. wears off quickly, and for me it wasn't all for the best. Some people say Washington is a small town and in some ways, it certainly is. But I can't say it preaches or practices real small-town values. Neither are Washington's weaknesses unique to Washington. Whether it's Hollywood's entertainment industry or New York's financial sector, big cities have their own cultures and they tend to be about elbows and advancement. I found being a congressman was quite a heady cup of wine, and it wasn't long before the small-town lessons and motivation to serve became blurred. I admittedly let the big city inflate my ego.

I had to lose a run for the U.S. Senate to step back and remember that service means more than a title, that relationships matter more than the office you hold, and that marriage, faith and family have greater staying power than headlines. This is what led me back to my hometown and a career working to bring these values of service back into my private and public lives. While public service is my calling and my career, I firmly believe that the lessons I have learned are relevant not just to those of us who seek public service careers, but also to so many other spheres of our lives. Because in just about everything we do and every profession, there's room to serve and there's always an opportunity to get better at it.

The lessons I share in this book are lessons that I came by honestly and, in some cases, after some pretty hard knocks. But the experiences I've had over the years and the people I've met from all walks of life who taught me their hard-earned wisdom, from world-famous leaders to more private individuals, have enabled me to navigate the heady rush of success and the bitter disappointment of defeat. (The woman I married has been my greatest teacher.) I've learned about love and loss, service and leadership, and hope to impart some of the same teachings that have driven, defined and at times dogged me throughout my life.

This book draws on what I've learned from my hometown, as well as experiences in public service. It's what I think of as *Chicken Soup for the "Political" Soul,* a self-help book for public servants and leaders, and for others who want to make a difference. I hope these lessons reveal effective ways to serve, in whatever capacity that may be. Maybe you are active in the local Chamber of Commerce or United Way, or perhaps you are running for public office yourself. Maybe you're a doctor, nurse or farmer, a community volunteer, or work for a company that helps people improve their quality of life. All of this, in some way, is a form of service. And that, ultimately, is what this book is about—a guide to help us all become better servants and in turn, better leaders. This is not a philosophical book nor an autobiography. It will be, I hope, a deeply practical book.

People tend to either mythologize or patronize those of us in "the heartland." My goal is to avoid doing either. Instead, from those amber waves of grain—and sugar beets and many other crops—I'd like to extract a grain of truth about small-town values. Truths about community and the obligations we owe to one another; truths about resilience, humility and hard work.

Those who live in small towns, I've found, have a good bit to share to help all of us on our paths. I have often said that in a very real sense, from our factories and farms to our churches and schools, Michigan is America. And our small towns play a big role.

I've been fortunate to cross paths with presidents of the United States and their Cabinet members, as well as Fortune 500 chief executives. Yet I still firmly believe that everything I learned about public service and leadership, I picked up in my hometown of Midland. Everything I am goes back to being a small-town boy. And everything one needs to know flows from the small town values that make us who we are. I hope the lessons and values shared on the following pages also will help you in some small way, on your journey through life.

Bill Schuette

Midland, Michigan

2015

ACKNOWLEDGMENTS

As Ringo Starr, one of the Beatles, proclaimed, "It Don't Come Easy."

He's right.

Writing a book isn't easy, it turns out. It takes a lot of encouragement from family and friends to get the final manuscript across the finish line.

My marvelous wife Cynthia, and our children Heidi and Bill, have been extremely supportive throughout this entire process. They have been my best and most constructive critics and my most loving and helpful editors. Thank you and I love you. Cynthia's dad, Carl E. Grebe, is an exceptional man. He is 96 years old, a World War II fighter pilot and a true example of service to our nation.

My mom, Esther Schuette Gerstacker; my dad, William H. Schuette; and my step-father, Carl A. Gerstacker, had a love for Midland and a commitment to family and hometowns that are the foundation of so many lessons in this book. My sisters Sandra, Gretchen and step-sister Lisa have been patient with me and helped in so many ways, for so many years. I love you, too.

My longtime, great friends, Tom Ludington, a brilliant federal judge, and Dave Camp, an outstanding congressman, are present throughout this book and have been and are a constant presence in my life. They know more stories ...

Growing up in Midland, Mike Driver was the older brother I never had. He helped me in every sport imaginable and to this day provides sound counsel and policy advice. Thanks, Mike.

David Johns was like a brother to me in junior high school, high school and college. He spent a lot of time at the Schuettes over the years and was a member of our family. While the geography that separates us is vast – David lives in Australia with his wife, Jude – he and I learned together the values of teamwork and discipline on and off the athletic fields.

Rusty Hills, a valued friend and a man with a gift of words, letters and communication, has listened to my stories for years now. Rusty was the driving force in managing this project and making our publishing timetable. Thank you, Iron Mountain.

Sarah Opperman, a skilled professional and writer, took my lessons, my stories and brought them to the page with energy and life. Her work has been beautiful.

Alan Ott, my dear friend and a family counselor to so many in Midland, as well as a banking visionary and community leader, has helped put people and projects together in Midland for decades. Thanks to Alan and Jean for teaching me many lessons, including the "Art of Peanut Brittle."

Andrew Liveris, a terrific friend, was a great role model in writing *Big Lessons* and our mutual friend Matt Davis had a guiding hand throughout.

I am fortunate to receive both counsel and correction from Peter Secchia. Peter is a former Ambassador to Italy, a leading philanthropist in West Michigan, a successful businessman and a sage Republican leader, advisor and friend. Whether he takes you to the woodshed or a football game, he is a generous and big-hearted guy. Thanks, Peter.

Dave Nicholson had more to do with this book than he may realize. Thank you for your friendship and for always being ready to help and offer an encouraging word.

Jim Barrett, a special friend, confidante and advisor, thanks for your kindness and leadership.

Dennis Starner saw many of these lessons firsthand. Thanks for your decades of friendship.

Lori Gay, Melissa Anderson, and Carter Bundy have made a big difference in *Big Lessons*. Thank you.

I deeply appreciate the sentiments expressed by Mark Dantonio. Mark is a coaches' coach, a rock-solid guy and an exceptional role model as a father, husband and leader. A true friend.

A special word of thanks to Barbara Bush, Jim Baker, Betsy DeVos, James Craig, and Keith Pretty for their warmth and kindness and years of support, encouragement and friendship. Their individual and collective participation in the production of this book provided me with lift and positivity at a crucial moment when manuscript deadlines were looming.

A warm thanks as well to Rafe Sagalyn, a talented agent, whose expertise helped get *Big Lessons* published.

And finally, Susan Bays of Arbutus Press, my publisher from Northern Michigan and a new friend, who deftly guided me through the production process. Thanks for your endurance.

My sincere and heartfelt thanks to all of you, and so many others, for helping to make this book a reality.

INTRODUCTION

MIDLAND AND ME

"No, I cannot forget where it is that I come from
I cannot forget the people who love me
Yeah, I can be myself here in this small town
And people let me be just what I want to be."
—*John Mellencamp, "Small Town"*

Midland is a town of about 40,000, nestled on the mitt-shaped map of Michigan, right between the thumb and the rest of the fingers.

If Midland helped make me who I am, what made Midland into Midland was brine. In 1890, a young Canadian chemist named Herbert Henry Dow rented a barn in the flatlands, gunned an old flour mill steam engine, and created a new process for extracting bromide from brine (bromide being widely used back then as a sedative). Seven years later, The Dow Chemical Company (Dow) was founded. Over the next century, Dow produced chemicals, plastics and agricultural products, growing to become one of the largest chemical companies in the world. From the Grace A. Dow Memorial Library, to the Single-A baseball Dow Diamond, to my alma mater, Midland Dow High School, Dow was also the center of the world for many Midland residents.

As a child, Dow loomed even larger in my life. My father, William H. (Bill) Schuette, was a Depression-era kid from Cleveland, the son of schoolteachers. He married his high school sweetheart, Esther Little, and they came to Midland in 1941 so my dad could work for Dow. My dad rose to become a member of Dow's Board of Directors at the remarkably young age of 45. He died of a heart attack just two years later in 1959, leaving my mother to raise my two older sisters, Sandra and Gretchen, and me. I was only six years old.

Sixteen years later, when I was a college junior, a smart guy named Carl Gerstacker, who served as Dow's chairman for a decade and a half, married my mother. So for me and Midland, Dow Chemical, as well as a sister corporation, Dow Corning, were and remain a constant presence, the region's largest employers and loyal civic partners.

Midland was a stable, relatively tranquil place to come of age. We had clean streets and beautiful churches (and still do). A pickup basketball game was a neighborhood affair, often at our house. We played in the garage when there was too much snow to play in the driveway (a driveway, incidentally, that was my responsibility to shovel in the winter). Dow provided good jobs and good salaries, as well as the contributions and muscle behind most local civic institutions.

In 2010, *Forbes* magazine named Midland one of the "Best Small Cities To Raise a Family," which is not bad for an old lumber town—and growing up, it certainly felt that way. (We were also proud when Midland was chosen "Best Tennis

Town" by the U.S. Tennis Association in 2009.) Being largely white and Protestant, Midland wasn't especially diverse, but it was fairly egalitarian—after all, nearly everyone was somehow connected to Dow and Dow Corning. Notably, their top executives tended to live modestly, participate actively and give generously.

Everyone I knew reinforced the notion that Midland was about working hard and giving back. Living there meant a strong work ethic, studying late and staying out of trouble. (I'll admit I wasn't always successful, but these values were constantly reinforced.)

One person instrumental in teaching me those values was a neighbor, Margaret Ann (Ranny) Riecker. The granddaughter of Herbert H. Dow, Ranny was tough, kind and wonderful, a woman who survived a couple bouts with cancer and many more bouts with political opponents. As a Republican National Committeewoman from Michigan, she was a force in Republican politics, advising former Governors George Romney and Bill Milliken, and former U.S. Senator Robert Griffin, in their campaigns.

Ranny was a beloved fixture of the community until she passed away in April 2014. But back when I was in junior high, she was my first boss and I was just her lawn boy, the one she'd kid about pulling out all her begonias instead of all her weeds. Somewhere amid all the yard work—and I certainly remember quite a bit of grass cutting and leaf raking—Ranny found time to fill my head with dreams of politics and public service.

Dave Camp and me, two neighbor kids, flanking Ranny Riecker at a breakfast in Midland in May 2011.
(Photo credit: The Herbert H. and Grace A. Dow Foundation.)

I was incredibly blessed to meet with her to discuss politics and how to build Midland, and I'll always treasure her wisdom and warmth. I visited with Ranny just days before she passed away to thank her for her life-long friendship and mentoring, and promising to continue her dream of renovating the downtown area of Midland. She asked about my Attorney General re-election campaign, listened, smiled and then in typical Ranny style, instructed me, "In November, go kick some ass." Yes, ma'am.

Ever since my mother and sisters came up with the slogan, "Billy Schuette Will Be on Duty for You," for an elementary school student council race, I'd been keen on running for office. (Decades later, after my incredible campaign consultants Susan and Jay Bryant, independently came up with a similar slogan we discovered note cards bearing that slogan from my first election for student council secretary.)

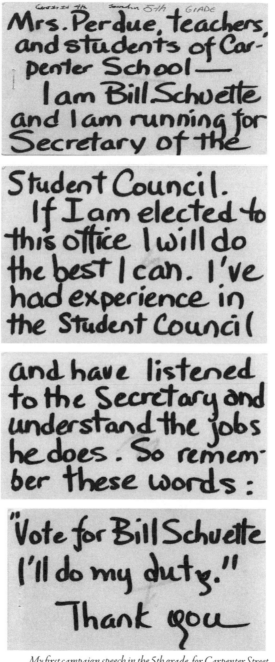

Mrs. Perdue, teachers, and students of Carpenter School —
I am Bill Schuette and I am running for Secretary of the Student Council.
If I am elected to this office I will do the best I can. I've had experience in the Student Council and have listened to the Secretary and understand the jobs he does. So remember these words:
"Vote for Bill Schuette I'll do my duty."
Thank you

My first campaign speech in the 5th grade, for Carpenter Street Elementary School Student Council secretary. The "Bill Schuette - On Duty" slogan was first used during this critical campaign. (Credit: Bill Schuette)

I felt the pull of politics and public service in part because I liked people, and in part because I wanted to do something that would have made my father proud. Subconsciously, I know I was afraid I'd never surpass his accomplishments in business. But I hoped to be equally successful in some way. Whatever the exact reason, after all those years listening as Ranny and her husband John Riecker shared stories with me of their other political friends, I was hooked.

Nor was I alone. One of my best friends was Dave Camp, who recently retired from my old congressional seat after 24 exemplary years of serving Michigan in Congress. He lived next door to Ranny, and the two of us would bike around the neighborhood gathering signatures to become precinct delegates to Republican state conventions. Later, I attended Georgetown University's School of Foreign Service and went on to the University of San Francisco School of Law. With Ranny's encouragement and a few phone calls, I worked for my then-Congressman Al Cederberg and assisted on several presidential campaigns, including Gerald Ford's 1976 campaign, George H.W. Bush's 1979-1980 primary campaign, and Ronald Reagan's 1980 campaign.

Along the way, I had the great privilege to see brilliant political operatives like James A. Baker III up close, to chauffeur the future President George H.W. Bush and to play regular basketball games with his sons, including a few young guys named W. (George W.) and Jeb. Some of the most important political lessons I learned came from working with and watching these men who would go on to become presidents and statesmen.

Jim Baker, a dear friend, political mentor and public service role model, at a luncheon in Grand Rapids, Michigan in 2014. Jim and I serve on the Gerald R. Ford Presidential Foundation. (Photo credit: Bill Schuette)

Jim Baker, for instance, had a mind like a steel trap, but he wasn't arrogant or cold. I worked for him on Gerald Ford's 1976 presidential campaign. Despite being a powerful man and future secretary of state, he treated his subordinates— young guys like me—with respect. If you went up against him though, you were going to lose. Even if it was a narrow victory, afterwards he'd say in that Texas drawl, "Bill, a win is a win is a win." He had perspective and heart.

It was a heady life, and I couldn't wait to make it my own. I wanted to win, too. After a few years practicing law in a local law firm, I filed to run for the U.S. House of Representatives. I was not quite 30 years old, and had spent the Memorial Day weekend before I announced watching *Star Wars: Return of the Jedi*. The movie seemed an apt metaphor for the uphill battle I faced.

More will be said on that first campaign later, but suffice it to say that a young man trudging through farmers' fields in loafers was not the odds-on favorite to unseat the popular Democratic incumbent, Rep. Don Albosta, a successful farmer in the largely rural district. I was such an underdog that people hardly stopped to talk to me, so I began pouring them coffee at every event just to have a chance to introduce myself. Somehow, with incredible help from my family, a core group of friends and some grit—not to mention capitalizing on the perception that the incumbent had "Gone Washington"— I overcame Albosta's huge lead and eked out a victory by just over a thousand votes. Baker had organized a visit by President Reagan the Friday prior to the Tuesday election, which was the critical boost I needed. After I survived a close recount, they jokingly called me "Landslide Schuette." I was riding high.

When I arrived in Congress, I learned the ropes and made sure to get myself on the House Agriculture Committee. In a rebuke to farmers, my opponent had left the committee, so I had promised voters that I would make it my priority. I kept my nose to the grindstone. But while I worked hard on the issues, I didn't work hard enough to build relationships. In fact, my transparent ambition turned off a lot of my fellow House members, especially in the Michigan delegation. At the time, however, I didn't much care. I was trying to survive, trying to climb higher and didn't recognize that not all ladders actually lead up.

In 1986, Don Albosta challenged me to a rematch and it was an ugly one. As the incumbent, I was no longer an underdog, strictly speaking. We both had name recognition and I now had a voting record to defend. But I pulled it out once more, nearly quadrupling my margin of victory to some 4,000 votes.

Two years later, I won again—this time in a real landslide. I was getting good at this. My approval ratings were high and my congressional office was clicking on all cylinders. Powerful people took my phone calls and invited me to the best parties. I'd even been named a "Hunk of the Hill." Before long, I started thinking, "Now may be the time to make the jump." If I was this popular and effective in one corner of the Michigan mitt, why not represent the whole thing? And why stop there?

To readers familiar with Greek tragedy, this is where humility quickly turned to hubris.

In this particular case, the facilitator of my fall would be a two-term U.S. senator with strong approval ratings, money in the bank and a willingness to bury his opponents —U.S. Senator Carl Milton Levin.

Don't let the kindly eyeglasses fool you; Levin was a brawler. "A tough city politician," as my campaign manager, Doug McAuliffe, described him. Levin first won an election to the U.S. Senate by knocking off Robert Griffin, a friend of Ranny Riecker's who was the Senate Republican Minority Whip and a former WWII infantryman. In 1984, the year I was first elected to the House, Levin dispatched Jack Lousma, an ex-astronaut, after a video revealed him telling Japanese businessmen that he owned a Toyota—a cardinal sin in Detroit at that time.

Levin was really something, yet after three terms in the House, he was the man I'd decided to beat. After all, I didn't lose elections. My stepfather vehemently tried to dissuade me, but I ignored his warnings. From a political standpoint, I should have heeded his advice and stayed in the House. As the legendary UCLA basketball coach John Wooden always said, "Be quick, but don't hurry." I was in a hurry.

The uphill battle to unseat Levin soon became apparent to anyone watching, though only gradually to me. As one Associated Press writer put it, "To date, the advantage has been all Levin's in his campaign for re-election." Levin raised four times as much as I, and used that huge cash advantage to run TV ads defining me before I could introduce myself to the voters.

A month away from the election, Levin was trouncing me 60-26 in the polls. More than one-third of Michigan voters had no idea I existed. Having made little effort to reach out and build relationships with Michigan's other members of Congress, few of my colleagues made much effort to campaign for me. I really can't say I blamed them.

But remembering my first, come-from-behind win, I compared myself to the NBA champion Detroit Pistons, thinking I could win the game in the final seconds. By then, even though I knew the likely outcome when I went home each night, I put on a good show in public, brashly reminding reporters already writing my obituary that, "The graveyards out there are littered with the bodies of candidates who were ahead in September and October and lost in November."

Levin would not be joining them. This time, there was no closing the gap. I lost, and I lost badly. For the whole campaign, Levin had run brutally effective TV ads. Those final few weeks, even when it was painfully clear I'd lose, he kept running them. The way I saw it, Levin was determined to beat me so badly I'd be finished in Michigan politics. My campaign was out of cash and I borrowed money from my local bank—again, against my stepfather's wishes—just to fight back. I knew I was out of gas.

I can still remember the election night phone call in vivid, brutal detail. Years later, when Levin announced his retirement in 2013, I praised his years of service and never brought up the 1990 race.

Having never lost anything of that magnitude before, my Senate race was extremely painful, both publicly and privately. It seriously damaged my relationship with my stepfather, and my mother was torn between him and me. It left me wondering what in the world I was going to do with my life. The day after that race, exhausted and deeply in debt, I wondered if there was a road back.

So I went home, back to Midland.

In returning to my roots, somehow, I picked myself up. As New Orleans Saints quarterback Drew Brees said in a December 2014 *The Times-Picayune* story, "Man, you've got to have short-term memory – good or bad. It's all about the next play and the next opportunity." In other words, when you throw an interception, you've got to get up, dust yourself off and throw some touchdowns.

During the campaign, I'd rekindled a relationship with someone from my childhood neighborhood, a girl who had ignored me for 20 years as we stood at the same bus stop and attended the same elementary, junior high and high schools. When we met again, Cynthia Grebe was a TV anchor in Grand Rapids. Had I not run for the U.S. Senate, I remain convinced that I would not have found the woman who would help me navigate the road of family, faith, relationships and service.

Cynthia was a clear and shining ray of hope. Fourteen years before President Barack Obama spoke about the *Audacity of Hope* during the 2004 Democratic Convention, I had my own personal audacity of hope to ask this accomplished news anchor, at the peak of her profession, to marry me—a guy who'd just lost a Senate race and had no job. My hope was that she would say yes. A few days after I lost, she did.

My fiancé Cynthia (third from left), with newsroom colleagues on her last day at WOTV-8, Grand Rapids, January 1991. (Photo credit: Cynthia Grebe Schuette)

Cynthia decided to leave the newsroom, and I was offered the position of Agriculture Director in the administration of Michigan's then-newly elected Governor John Engler. All those hours studying agricultural issues came in handy. While I was Ag Director, Cynthia and I founded the Michigan Harvest Gathering, a food drive that has raised more than $9.3 million and 9.5 million pounds of food for the hungry over the past 24 years. During the early days of this effort to raise food and funds for Michigan's food banks, we also welcomed our children, Heidi and Bill.

A few years later, Midland's seat in the Michigan Senate opened up. Some people were shocked that anyone would go from the U.S. Congress—"The Show"—to our state Legislature in Lansing, but I saw it as another pathway to service and maybe "a shot at redemption," as Paul Simon once sang. I ran, won and spent the next decade as state senator relearning how to build relationships, to legislate and to lead by serving first—listening hard to the people around me, not to my own ambition.

In 2002, I was elected a judge of the Michigan Court of Appeals, meaning I'd served in every branch of government before age 50. Before long, I was running to become Michigan's Attorney General, and on January 1, 2011, I was sworn in. That honor and responsibility would be repeated on January 1, 2015.

From Ranny Riecker's lawn to the Capitol Dome, from the sting of defeat to the amazement of marriage and the thrill of fatherhood, I've gotten my shot at service, disappointment and redemption. I've learned a lot along the way. And all these decades later—literally and metaphorically—my home is still in Midland, and I still am committed to remain on duty.

LESSON 1

Work Hard.
Then Work Harder.

"A hungry dog hunts a little harder."

—Al Quick, former Midland Dow High School football coach

I announced I was running for U.S. Congress just after Memorial Day, 1983. At the time, Michigan's 10th District was the second largest congressional district east of the Mississippi River. With a small group of wonderful friends, we had spent the Memorial Day weekend stuffing, stamping and folding about 4,000 letters, which John Riecker had helped draft, announcing my candidacy. I had been planning this run since right after the 1982 election, which I'd wisely but oh-so-anxiously decided against entering. Since January, I'd been building the campaign and courting supporters, while trying to avoid tipping off anyone that I was going to run, including the GOP's previous candidate, a fine man who was planning to try again.

I shouldn't have worried. My entrance into the race answered the age-old Zen riddle: "If a young whippersnapper announces his congressional campaign, and nobody seems to notice, is he still a candidate?"

Beyond a handful of stalwarts within the Republican organization, the announcement made hardly a ripple. My name was hard to pronounce, no one had heard of me and even fewer cared. It was difficult to get invited to speak at events and when I did, no one recognized me anyway. The Midland community knew I was running and gave me much-needed support in those early days, but that's only because small towns are like that. They look after their own.

While I was young and nearly invisible in the district, my opponent, incumbent Rep. Don Albosta, was neither of those things. Albosta was a political giant in our part of the state. He was a big, gruff farmer with all the advantages of an incumbent congressman. Six years earlier, in 1978, he'd upset Al Cederberg, the 26-year veteran for whom I'd interned. Farmers had trusted Albosta as one of their own, and he knew how to "talk local" to the Chamber of Commerce. In a district that loved then-President Ronald Reagan, Albosta boasted that he was "more popular than Reagan." It certainly seemed that way, though concerns about his leaving the Agriculture Committee and his grandstanding investigation of Reagan's alleged use of debate crib sheets were starting to make voters think twice.

Two months before Election Day, our internal polling had me 19 points down. A month later, it was 12 points—still double digits. Sounding more confident than I felt, I told one reporter, "We're going to be an underdog. It's going to be close, it's going to be tight, but we're going to win."

Eventually, I came to realize that being the underdog could be an asset. It kept me hungry; it kept me listening carefully and working hard. And in the end, it has helped me become a better servant leader.

Coffee Pot Leadership

What I would do was this: I would go into every Kiwanis and Rotary Club meeting, every Farm Bureau event and every roadside coffee shop. There were a lot more of those back then, dotting the main roads through small towns like gas stations. Whether it was the YMCA in Owosso or the old Ranch House Restaurant in Beaverton, I'd introduce myself, politely wrest the coffee pot from the staff, and start serving piping-hot coffee—doing my very best to hit the cup more often than someone's lap. (I like to say that I want to make an impression on people, but not on their skirt, shirt or trousers.)

Pouring coffee became my signature. In a gentle way, it got people to say hello when they might otherwise have ignored me. And it forced me to say hello too, instead of sitting or standing around with my hands in my pockets. It also gave me an excuse to talk with and learn from a lot of different people. Over time, as I started seeing familiar faces, I became more comfortable in my own skin, and more at ease discussing the problems and challenges they faced, as well as their hopes and dreams for their families, their businesses and their communities.

Pouring coffee -- regular and decaf, of course -- at the Grand Traverse Republican Party breakfast, just before the Cherry Parade in Traverse City, July 2014. (Photo credit: Carter Bundy)

I'll admit that initially the move was a simple tactic to introduce myself. But then something happened. I'd lean over someone's cup, and he'd start telling me how he'd had to sell the farm that had been in his family for generations.

Or a woman would shake my hand and then tell me about her concern that she couldn't afford to send her daughter to college. People would inform me that property taxes were too high. Or they'd ask: "Where are the jobs?"

I poured coffee; they poured out their stories and advice.

I'd always liked people, and on the deepest, most fundamental level, I was running for office because I wanted to help and serve. But it was during those 18 months of serving coffee—cup by cup and person by person—that their issues became real to me, and my job as a servant leader became clear. Approaching a person like that, open-minded and wanting to hear what they have to say, is a humbling experience. You realize that your preconceptions aren't always right. I wanted to get to Congress to do something for the people who had shared their dreams and concerns with me.

Intently listening was a necessity when I was the heavy underdog, but I've found it just as essential even when—especially when—things are going well. Too often, we think that leadership is top-down, something that happens when a bunch of politicians or executives convene around a conference room table. It's really not. Leadership begins in the kitchen—or the coffee shop—and obvious as it sounds, it takes a lot of listening and hard work.

Working Hard Is a Talent

There are many leaders, from the boardroom to the basketball court, who understand what I like to call "Coffee Pot Leadership." These leaders aren't always the flashiest, but what they do works. And what they do is listen well, work their tails off and take nothing for granted.

Take Tom Izzo, currently the head coach of Michigan State University's men's basketball team. Izzo was born in Iron Mountain, in Michigan's Upper Peninsula, and attended Northern Michigan University. Northern Michigan is a Division II school, but folks still doubted that Izzo could play on the basketball team. He needed a letter from his high school coach just for the opportunity to walk on. But by senior year, Izzo was team captain and an All-American athlete.

After graduation, Izzo stayed on as a graduate assistant with the basketball program. Izzo didn't get a Division I job until 1983, when Michigan State hired him as an assistant. Even then, he wasn't named head coach until 1995. But Izzo's unflagging dedication and ability to keep his nose to the grindstone paid off in the end. An eight-time National Coach of the Year, Izzo has now won one NCAA championship, enjoyed seven Final Four appearances, sixteen consecutive NCAA tournament bids, and is the longest-serving active Big Ten men's basketball coach.

Despite all that success, Izzo hasn't forgotten what got him to where he is: humility, nonstop hard work, and a refusal to give in when the going got tough. In 2012, one of his players told *The New York Times*, "He coaches every single player, every single minute as if it's a close game. That's hard for guys to understand sometimes. 'Coach, we're up by 30 points, why are you screaming and hollering?' Well, he's preparing for down the road." That's the measure of a true leader—not just how hard they work when they're down, but whether they work just as hard when they're up.

Or, as Thomas Edison famously wrote and my mother often paraphrased, "Genius is one percent inspiration and ninety-nine percent perspiration."

Of course, that mindset becomes even more crucial in times of crisis. I remember in 2009, when The Dow Chemical Company was on the verge of completing a major deal with Kuwait, as well as a deal to acquire Rohm and Haas. Everything was on track until unexpectedly, Kuwait pulled out of the deal.

Investors panicked. The stock plummeted. Dow teetered on the edge of survival. Chairman and CEO Andrew Liveris and his team righted the ship through a painstaking, grind-it-out effort that is a hallmark of successful leadership. Dow created a number of small teams, each tasked with tackling different parts of the crisis. After three long months, the intensive work salvaged the Rohm and Haas deal and stabilized the company.

These are the lessons that we're taught in our hometowns. That there's no substitute for sweat. That no task is beneath you and nothing comes without a whole lot of effort and a healthy dose of elbow grease. I learned that lesson well. From Ranny Riecker's lawn boy, I also was the head potato boy when the new Ponderosa Steak House opened in town in 1971, and did construction work in Colorado one summer on college break. In a political race or just about any other situation, a sense of entitlement can get you knocked senseless. Instead, what real servant leaders do is buckle down, hop in the trenches with their team, and figure out how to get past whatever obstacles life throws their way.

If you do that when you're up and when you're down, on days when you're feeling good and on days when it's uphill sledding, you'll find yourself connecting to the people around you a lot better. You'll see solutions you hadn't seen before. You'll develop a whole new perspective on yourself, your career and the organizations you belong to and manage.

So roll up your sleeves, reach for the coffee pot, listen carefully and work hard. That's leadership.

LESSON 2

Don't Be a Ball Hog

"When you get into the end zone, act like you've been there before."

—Vince Lombardi

October 1, 1932: Game 3 of the World Series. It's the top of the fifth inning, the score all tied up at four runs apiece. The Chicago Cubs are heckling Babe Ruth, the New York Yankees' legendary slugger, as he steps up to the plate. Ruth points to the center field bleachers—"calling" his shot—then blasts the ball into them, sending Wrigley Field into shock and the Yankees on to the World Series title.

Ruth's "called shot"—the 15th and final home run of his playoff career—is a dramatic, even iconic, moment in sports history. It's also precisely the wrong way for most of the rest of us to proceed in politics and in life. The Bambino could pull it off. But for the rest of us, calling your shot—that is, suggesting (usually wrongly) your own superiority—can only hurt relationships and undermine success.

These days, unfortunately, there are a lot of individuals out there acting like Ruth, and I don't mean that they're hitting .342. We seem to live in an era in which narcissism is not only accepted, but encouraged and celebrated. Inside the Beltway, the political consultant Kevin Madden has dubbed this the "firstnamelastname-dot-com syndrome," where everybody is

43

their own brand and every brand has to beat the others. To varying degrees, that's true outside Washington, D.C., too. We have, literally at our fingertips, technologies that tempt us and apps that enable us to make it "all about us." Social networks like Facebook and Twitter—while valuable in many ways—also drive a culture in which every passing thought, everything you "like" and do, is instantaneously broadcast to an audience doing the same thing. Most of us want Babe Ruth's swagger, but we possess none of his swing.

Things are a little different in the small towns where many of us were raised. People who are self-absorbed or "putting on airs" sure don't go very far. At the very least, they probably get a stern talking-to. Away from the bright lights of the big cities, we judge a person's character by how they act, not by the number of "Retweets" they accumulate on Twitter. While I don't mean to suggest that small towns hold all the answers to modern life, I suspect we'd do ourselves and society a lot of good by reacquainting ourselves with the values taught by our families and friends.

In my own hometown, I have had the great fortune to grow up with a man who lives and breathes those values— Alan Ott. Al is a retired banker and a quiet powerhouse of a man, which is one of the reasons he's been a lifelong role model for me and so many others. It's no contradiction to say that the man is the Babe Ruth of service and humility.

Al was born in the small town of Manistique in Michigan's Upper Peninsula. He started his career as an entry-level teller at a local bank in Clare, another small town in mid-Michigan, where he met and married Jean, a fellow teller. For a long time, Al was president of Midland's Chemical Bank, having worked his way up after starting out as a cashier. As Chemical Bank expanded across the state under his leadership, it included the purchase of that small bank in Clare. Al served in the Korean War, and he's never stopped serving since. He could always tell the corporate titans in town, including my stepfather, when they were wrong and then guide the discussion toward how to solve whatever the problem was.

Midland's Dow Diamond, our top-shelf baseball stadium and home of the Great Lakes Loons, a Single A team of the Los Angeles Dodgers.(Photo credit:Nick Anderson/Great Lakes Loons)

I remember when Bill Stavropoulos, then Chairman of the Board of The Dow Chemical Company, led the effort to create a minor league baseball team and stadium in Midland a decade ago. It was his inspiration to purchase and move a baseball team from Battle Creek to Midland, and to build a state-of-the-art ballpark, creating a regional family-oriented attraction that not only entertains, but also gives back to the community. His passionate leadership, as well as the contributions of local businesses and foundations, is what small-town civic leadership is all about. At the same time, Al quietly made sure the local foundations and organizations contributed, as well. He has a way of pulling people together and building support—using persuasion, not intimidation— and he still greases the skids for virtually every major project in town.

Now in his 80s, Al is "Mr. Midland," the behind-the-scenes leader and a valued and trusted advisor for community organizations throughout mid-Michigan. I tried to get him to smile at a photo shoot for our foundation not long ago. "Bill," he said quietly, but with a twinkle in his eye, "I can't smile; I'm a banker." He solves problems, fixes things and repairs relationships. And when you can do things like that, communities blossom. They're stronger and richer in every sense of the word. His name isn't plastered on every newspaper but, in so many ways, his expertise, dedication and vision continue to influence our small town. He is a teacher, advisor and friend. Cynthia encourages me to see Al every week, and some of the best moments of my week are when I spend time with him.

We all know an "Alan Ott." They're the men and women who generously contribute their time and talent, often behind the scenes or even anonymously. They're the hardware store owner whose greatest joy is coaching Little League and the neighbor who volunteers to clean up the local park. They deftly guide our churches, civic organizations and families through the good times and the bad, offering sage advice, honesty and unwavering support. And if we work very hard, with a little luck, each of us might be described the same way.

Be Humble — or Be Humbled

Although I grew up with these values and tried to live them personally, the importance of humility can be easily forgotten—especially when we stray too far from our small towns. I know; I learned the hard way. As a 31-year-old, first-term congressman, I got caught up in the excitement of Washington. I returned to the city where, just a decade earlier, I had been a college student. It was a dream come true. I learned that if you're not careful, your ego can inflate to the size of the Capitol Dome. I worked hard, but I was also impatient and along the way forgot an important lesson from home—relationships. Caught up in the work and glamour of the role, I took those relationships for granted, even with my colleagues in the Michigan congressional delegation.

Former Michigan Governor George Romney, leading the applause following my nomination for U.S. Senate at the 1990 Michigan Republican Convention in Detroit. (Photo credit: Bill Schuette)

Michigan native son and 2012 Republican nominee for president, Mitt Romney attending a fundraiser with Cynthia and me in June 2014 for my Michigan Attorney General re-election campaign. (Photo credit: Carter Bundy)

In 1988, just four years after getting elected and as I was gearing up for my 1990 U.S. Senate race, my campaign ran a television advertisement to broaden my name recognition in Michigan. And boy, was it a beauty. There was magnificent footage of cornfields, the sun setting behind a grain silo emblazoned with the American flag and a tagline, "Bill Schuette, Michigan's Congressman." The only problem? There were 17 other members of Congress from Michigan. Not surprisingly, they weren't particularly pleased. A lot of them rightly thought that—after years of service to their state—they, too, were Michigan's congressmen. Many were cool to requests for support during my campaign and I don't blame them. It was not very "Ott."

It was a strong reminder of those lessons I had learned back home—lessons about the importance of remaining humble, of building and respecting relationships, and of being sensitive to others. I've been lucky to maintain lifelong friendships, some dating back to grade school. But at the time, I wasn't mature enough to realize the damage that such an advertisement and my aggressive attitude would create. Now older and hopefully wiser, I look back at that hard-charging young man, shake my head and give thanks that time has sanded off at least some of my rougher edges.

Moore's Law: Don't Be a Ball Hog

Shortly after I was elected Attorney General in 2010, I attended a conference of the National Association of Attorneys General. While there, I met former Mississippi Attorney General Mike Moore at a reception. Mike's a diehard Democrat from the small town of Pascagoula, Mississippi. As we chatted, he cautioned me that, as Attorney General, my office would have enough high-profile drug busts and white-collar arrests to conduct a celebratory press conference every week. But he gently warned me not to get caught up in seeking constant attention.

"Don't be a ball hog," Mike said.

I call this bit of tried-and-true advice, "Moore's Law" (not to be confused with the better-known Moore's Law articulated by Intel co-founder Gordon E. Moore, which has something to do with transistors and the exponential increase in computing power). I thought about Mike's message a lot as I set up my office. It really resonated, in part because we all remember that kid—you know, the one who'd dribble the length of the court by himself when his teammates were wide open—and nobody liked him. I'd already made those sorts of missteps as a congressman, and hoped not to repeat my youthful mistakes. Moreover, I realized that many of us fall prey to self-promotion too—in sports, politics and business, and life in general.

So while the Attorney General's office certainly does generate plenty of press and aggressively communicates the various responsibilities of the nearly 500 men and women who serve Michigan each day, our team tries to follow Mike Moore's Law as best we can in the arena of government and public service. We're not perfect, but our office philosophy is to focus specifically on the issues and to share credit, making sure to quote others who are directly involved. And as Earvin

"Magic" Johnson said, "Everybody on a championship team doesn't get publicity, but everyone can say he's a champion."

Take, for instance, a new student safety initiative called OK2SAY. The idea came from Joanne Spry, then-superintendent of public schools in Cadillac, Michigan, who contacted me shortly after the Sandy Hook Elementary School shootings in December 2012. She said Michigan needed a system similar to the "Safe to Tell" program that was started in Colorado after the 1999 Columbine High School incident. According to federal studies, in most of the violent attacks that have tragically taken place in our schools, someone besides the offender—a classmate, a parent—was aware of the potential attack, but did not alert the proper authorities. Joanne rightly believed that we need to break the culture of silence and replace it with a shared commitment to safety.

OK2SAY has been a true collaborative effort. It began with Joanne's initiative, and grew to include strong bipartisan leadership by the Michigan Legislature, the Office of the Governor, our Department of the Attorney General, the Michigan State Police, and the Michigan Departments of Community Health, Education and Human Services, as well as associations and school districts across the state. The state Legislature also approved a $4 million appropriation to implement the initiative. It's this type of collaborative policy making that is most rewarding and more importantly, most effective.

Another great example of someone who shared the policy ball and developed effective and lasting solutions is

Jim Baker. I saw his skill again when he was Secretary of the Treasury and I was in Congress.

Baker played the leading role in the historic 1986 Tax Reform Act that closed loopholes and lowered tax rates. He knew that tax reform was critical for the country and important to then-President Reagan—so much so that Baker agreed to give up the arguably more powerful role of White House Chief of Staff to become Secretary of the Treasury. In that new role, Baker became a driving force, but not the only one, behind the reform effort. He recognized that reforming the tax code affected practically everyone in the country, so he consulted countless stakeholders, from Republicans Bob Packwood and Jack Kemp to Democrats Bill Bradley and Dan Rostenkowski. He empowered them all to advance the ball together until, as the journalists Jeffrey Birnbaum and Alan Murray write, "In the early hours of the morning on May 7, tax reform completed its transformation from the impossible to the inevitable."

When we share the ball—whether at the firm, within the political party, or across our state and nation—we can contribute individually while drawing on our colleagues' unique and varied strengths. Some of us see the big picture strategy; others have a greater technical grasp on a subject or a flair for defining and presenting an issue. But no matter what, we'll almost always be better off when we share the task—and the credit—with others. Sure, Babe Ruth was a tremendous player. But his team's name is the one emblazoned on the championship pennants at Yankee Stadium.

The No Bragging Zone

Then there's the ball hog's kissing cousin, the braggart. I try to avoid being over-sensitive to it, but I am occasionally troubled by the sheer volume of self-promotion and outright boasting present in our culture today. Today's society—especially online—seems to encourage us to broadcast how special we are.

Consider a counterexample—Warren Buffett. While Wall Street and Silicon Valley throw lavish, Gilded Age soirées (to which Washington insiders desperately want to be invited), Buffett shuns the high-priced toys and status symbols often associated with the wealthy. He's worth more than $40 billion, but lives in the same Omaha home he bought for $31,500 in 1958. He prefers hot dogs and cheeseburgers to caviar and foie gras, or as he put it to CNBC's Squawk Box, he'll eat anything he ate at his fifth birthday party and not much else. He has pledged to donate more than 99 percent of his wealth to philanthropy. "Too often, a vast collection of possessions ends up possessing its owner," Buffett said. "The asset I most value, aside from health, is interesting, diverse, and long-standing friends." With two dozen books published in a one-year period between 2012 and 2013 about Buffett's unique methods and lifestyle, his focus on substance over flash certainly has won him many admirers.

Of course, not all of us can be the "Oracle of Omaha" (or even the Oracle of Anywhere). But we can learn a lot from watching Buffett, and not just the latest stock tips. The generation that lived through the Great Depression, including my parents and many of my early mentors, was frugal. They'd known war and hardship, and they developed a deep distaste for ostentation. It's just how they lived their lives. And while a few may have taken it to the extreme, their attitudes and strong values reflect an important lesson for our generation and our children's.

My stepfather was a successful and prominent businessman, yet he never flaunted or advertised his wealth. My mother used to say, "Nothing goes to waste at Schuettes'." Casseroles made of leftovers were typical dinner fare. (I remain a big fan of casseroles, though oddly our children do not seem to have inherited this trait.) I can remember my stepfather giving me grief whenever I ordered a name-brand gin when we were out having dinner. He thought the house brand of gin was just fine, thank you very much. To this day, I think of him and smile when I occasionally order a tumbler of Tanqueray on ice. I try hard to be humble, but we're all still human.

This chapter ends where it started—in a town modest in both size and temperament, but not in accomplishment. A place where people work hard and take pride in that work, but don't flaunt their success or live larger than their means. Lesson Two is all about getting the job done, humbly and with the help and support of colleagues—whether it's playing ball, investing in a community or developing sound public policy. After all, they all require teamwork. There's no need and no room for ball hogs.

Don't Let Your Defeats Define You

"I've missed more than 9,000 shots in my career. I've lost almost 300 games. Twenty-six times, I've been entrusted to take the game-winning shot, and missed. I have failed over and over and over again in my life. And that is why I succeed."

—Michael Jordan

Boom and Bust

Sometimes, we set our sights a little too high, fall a bit short, and have to dust ourselves off and try again.

Growing up in Midland, it's a story we know all too well.

Take timber, for instance. The lumber barons from back East took one look at Michigan's sprawling white pine forests and predicted a timber boom that would last 500 years.

To fuel that boom they built railroads, sawmills and hotels; whole novels were set in the rough-and-tumble area near the Red Keg Saloon. Lured by the prospect of steady work, entire communities sprang up around Midland County.

But the boom didn't last 500 years, it lasted 50. By 1887, the boom had gone bust. The piles of logs waiting to go downriver—millions of feet at the height of the logging years—dwindled to nothing. Railroads sat idle. Logging gave way to limbo, which gave way to…well, what? Those few who remained weren't sure.

Then came Herbert H. Dow and his chemistry vision, and before they knew it, Midland was in the bromide business. As The Dow Chemical Company expanded and diversified over the next few decades, Midland County also had its economic ups and downs. It weathered, for example, the depression but in the 1930s experienced another brief boom—oil this time—before coming back down to earth. The point is that every time the people of Midland have had a challenge, they have toughed it out and transformed themselves to again succeed.

It's a neat lesson, isn't it? The resilience of a small town. They felled the trees, but never the people.

Lose One for the Gipper

In August 1976, my focus was on delegates at the National Republican Convention in Kansas City, not historical timberland along the Tittabawassee River. It was America's bicentennial, there was a presidential election going on, and the Republican Party—following then-President Richard Nixon's resignation—was working hard to rally the faithful.

I was for Gerald Ford, a Michigan man, but Ronald Reagan had been coming on strong all summer, firing up the conservative base. Within the GOP, tensions and nerves were running high. Going into the convention, Ford had maintained a narrow lead in the primaries and, we thought, in the delegate count. But high up in the bleachers of Kansas City's Kemper Arena, as an intern for Jim Baker, Ford's convention chieftain at the time—I could tell it was going to be a nail-biter.

In the end, Reagan lost narrowly on the first ballot by 117 votes. He was asked to offer some impromptu remarks, which he did. He said something about bold colors, not pale pastels, but what mattered to me at that moment was that I'd been working hard for Ford, and he'd just secured enough delegates to win. (In an ironic twist, after working with Ford to defeat Reagan in the 1976 primary, it was Reagan's 11th hour campaign appearance in Midland that helped push me over the top to victory in my 1984 congressional race.)

Some considered Reagan's concession speech to be his political farewell. After all, the man was already 65 at the time; how much of a career could he have left? He'd run in 1968 and lost. He'd run in 1976, coming extremely close to winning the Republican presidential nomination—and lost again. Stick a fork in him; Reagan was through.

As we all know, it didn't work out that way. Reagan got up off the mat. He conceded gracefully, worked doggedly and learned from his earlier missteps. Because he refused to let his defeats define him, four years later Reagan won the Republican nomination, the presidency and the hearts of millions of Americans. The long-gone loggers of Midland would have taken a look at the resilience of Ronald Reagan (born in an apartment above a bakery in Tampico, Illinois,

1908 population, 1500) and pronounced him "presidential timber."

Falling Backward Can Be a Good Thing

One and one-half decades later in 1990, I was the one conceding. It was a smaller stage, a lesser office and a far more decisive loss, but I had the same sick feeling that it was all over. While I wasn't alone—every one of the five Young Turks (first-time Republican candidates for the U.S. Senate) lost in this mid-year campaign— I felt I was washed up. Around the water coolers on Capitol Hill, "Pulling a Schuette" became the shorthand for someone who gave up a safe Congressional seat for an uphill battle against a tough, well-established incumbent U.S. Senator.

While I was uncertain about what the future might bring, I was indeed certain about two things. First, I did not want to be hanging around Washington, D.C., like the old Dusty Springfield song, just *"Wishin' and Hopin'"* about what could have happened if I had won. Second, and most importantly, I knew I was going to ask Cynthia Grebe to marry me.

So there I was, November 1990, days after the election. I was sitting in the parking lot of the Grand Rapids TV station waiting for Cynthia to finish work, worn out from a tough campaign and pretty down about my new professional status (or lack thereof). I received an unexpected call from then-President George H.W. Bush, consoling me on my defeat. (This is back when a mobile phone was a big, black contraption mounted in the car.) I asked, "How are you doing,

Mr. President?" And he said, "Well, it's a picture-perfect day here at Hobe Sound," the Bush family home in Florida. Then he said, "I think I'm going to go fishing." Not exactly what I needed to hear at that moment.

In contrast, it was a cold, rainy day in Grand Rapids and the foul weather mirrored my post-campaign mood. Sensing my unhappiness, the president said, "Bill, don't worry about the election. I lost my U.S. Senate race (in 1970 against Lloyd Bentsen), and things turned out OK for me."

Naturally, I had tremendous respect for Bush, whom I'd chauffeured during the presidential primaries in 1979 and 1980 and backed in his 1988 presidential campaign. They say you know who your true friends are because they show up on rainy days, and Bush certainly did. Moreover, he was taking the time to call when I had just lost an important race. I've never forgotten his kindness.

Still, at that moment I wasn't especially cheered by his pep talk. *Sure, Mr. President,* I thought. *You lost, but then you went on to be U.S. envoy to China, CIA director, chairman of the Republican National Committee—all these other opportunities.*

As I thought more about it after his call, I realized that Bush was right—things were going to turn out OK. We all find ourselves in these positions, sooner or later. We lose a job, or a spouse or an election. We fall short with our children. A town's entire livelihood may pack up and move away.

It's been said many times before, but there's truth in every truism. All of us will encounter adversity. It's what we learn from adversity—and how we respond to it—that matters. Or as Vince Lombardi said, "It's not whether you get knocked down, it's whether you get up." That realization is what allowed me to pick myself up and, to slowly bounce back. To refuse to let my defeat define me.

Just a few days after losing the Senate bid, I knelt down, lost my balance and actually fell over backward while proposing to Cynthia. Today, years later, I don't remember my political fall so much as my falling backward when I asked Cynthia to be my wife. She got me righted again then, and still does today.

The 1990 White House Christmas Party. President George H.W. Bush and First Lady Barbara Bush graciously meet and welcome my fiancé Cynthia. (Photo credit: George Bush Presidential Library Museum)

Review, Revise and Redefine

John Engler, governor at that time, threw me a political lifeline following the Senate race loss by appointing me the director of Michigan's Department of Agriculture. During the three years in this role, I worked to grow personally and professionally, to reinforce my hometown roots and values, and to focus on Michigan. I wanted to be better and do better. I wanted to serve the public better.

After three years at the Department of Agriculture, and having already served in the U.S. Congress, I took the unorthodox step of running for the Michigan Senate. I went to Lansing and our state capital to learn. To relearn, really, and to correct what I'd done wrong in the past. If I'd often been too ambitious and impatient in Congress, now I tried to actively cosponsor legislation and helped to start and host a monthly bipartisan breakfast group among Senate members. If I'd once sent out press releases touting my achievements, now I made sure the focus was first on the achievement itself, and then on others who were instrumental in the work.

The first time I got up to speak in the state Senate and asked to "revise and extend" my remarks—a common request in Congress, but not in Lansing—everybody laughed and gave me a much-deserved ribbing. But I got the hang of it. I found new purpose and new opportunities to serve mid-Michigan and the rest of the state.

I will never forget the pain of that ill-fated 1990 loss, but I learned from it and have worked hard in the years since. I have had the privilege since then to serve in Michigan's executive, legislative and judicial branches. I'm married to a wonderful woman and together we have two amazing children. We have raised our children in our hometown, a small community with strong values and decent, hard-working friends and neighbors.

The journey I took—from losing office to gaining a deeper sense of purpose—has been essential to my commitment to serve and to lead. Pretty much every successful public figure, in fact, has been knocked down a few times before he or she really succeeds.

But it's not just about getting back on the horse; it's about learning from the fall and riding the horse differently when you get back up.

Herbert H. Dow's first chemical venture in Canton, Ohio, went bankrupt within a year. His second, the Midland Chemical Company, forced him out. Townspeople took to calling him "Crazy Dow." But, it's what Dow biographer and dear friend Ned Brandt calls Dow's "degree from the school of hard knocks" that ultimately taught Dow how to perfect his chemistry and his company, and turn The Dow Chemical Company into the world leader it is today.

The late Steve Jobs, revered today for his uncanny ability to create technology we didn't even know we wanted, failed a lot, too. He dropped out of college, was forced out of Apple, failed when he started NeXT and failed when he founded Pixar. Each time, he learned from his mistakes.

As Jobs put it in his iconic 2005 Stanford University commencement address, none of his subsequent success "would have happened if I hadn't been fired from Apple. It was awful tasting medicine, but I guess the patient needed it. Sometimes life hits you in the head with a brick. Don't lose faith. I'm convinced that the only thing that kept me going was that I loved what I did."

Journalist and author Rick Newman calls these people "rebounders"—not because they're good basketball players, but because they bounce back. That ability—and need—to step back, reassess and then move forward again holds true for organizations as well.

Earvin "Magic" Johnson said it well: "For me, it always goes back to something I learned in basketball. There's winning and there's losing, and in life you have to know they both will happen. But what's never been acceptable to me is quitting."

In 2009, Ann Arbor-based Domino's Pizza was feeling the heat from the recession. Sales were decreasing worryingly and so was income. Customers thought their pizza tasted like "cardboard." A research firm confirmed what the company already knew: Domino's was dead last when it came to pizza preference among customers.

So the 50-year-old company reinvented itself.

Between 2009-2010, under the direction of Chairman David A. Brandon and his successor, President and CEO J. Patrick Doyle (another Midland native), Domino's responded directly to the complaints about their pizza quality, changing recipes and adding higher quality ingredients, while also improving and expanding items on the menu. Domino's also improved their already highly-regarded delivery service by creating an app that allowed customers to order online and track their order from the time it was placed to the time their food arrived at the door.

Customers responded enthusiastically. In the first quarter of 2010, the company reported a 14.3 percent increase in sales over the first quarter of 2009. Since then, Domino's has continued to post higher profits and sales, which has allowed the company to develop new stores at a faster pace. Today, they are close to overtaking Pizza Hut as the industry leader.

When the dominoes start to fall, it's easy to feel like everything is coming apart—your life, your career and your family situation. But at the same time, reflecting and reevaluating can help us rebuild just as readily, one tile on top of the other, until we are back and better than before.

Putting Family First

I know that's how I felt.

Like all those others, from Herbert H. Dow to Dave Brandon and Pat Doyle at Domino's, I reframed how I viewed that period of my life. Sure, I lost a political contest, but I never would have reunited with Cynthia if it hadn't been for the campaign. Adversity can lead to opportunity if you can see through the clutter.

At age 37, I basically started over, more focused on the things that really matter in life.

Before long, Cynthia and I were blessed with two incredible kids, Heidi and Bill. All the things I never got to do with my own Dad, I've had the good fortune to do with my own children. I've been able to attend Heidi's tennis matches and Bill's football, basketball and baseball games. I don't take for granted being able to share the big moments in their lives, and deeply treasure the joy of talking with them during the quiet moments too, when there's a shared joke or story, or when they might ask for some advice.

I just never dreamed some of those special times would include Kenny Chesney. As I think back, perhaps Cynthia and I put Kenny in play, though. Heidi was born in Lansing and I can remember that as a baby we would turn the radio to WITL, the local country music station, to calm her down when she was fussy. That's probably why she's still such a country music fan. Her favorite artist is Kenny Chesney, and over the years I've taken her to seven – yes, seven – of his concerts, sitting with her when she was young, and later hanging out in the back of the hall when she was a young teenager and didn't want Dad too close. And you know, I still like to listen to his music.

I just hope Cynthia and I are teaching the small town and sometimes hard-earned lessons to our children. When he was in high school, our son Bill was elected freshman class president. He then ran for sophomore class president; he lost. He ran for junior class president, and lost again. Senior year, he ran one last time, and—wouldn't you know it—Bill

Our family in Midland in 2013 (l to r): Bill, Heidi, me and Cynthia. (Photo credit: Morley Portraiture)

Schuette was elected senior class president of Midland Dow High School. While we were happy he won in his senior year, we are most proud of his tenacity and resilience. It will serve him well in life.

Nothing has been more important, or filled me with a greater sense of peace and purpose, than this time I've been blessed to spend with Cynthia, Heidi and Bill. Our children are, bar none, my greatest accomplishment—one I share proudly and humbly with Cynthia. My family has helped me bounce back and remind me why I really want to serve. They are the reason I get up every morning, and who I most look forward to seeing at the end of the day.

They also have helped me come to realize that, in the end, we're not remembered for our rejections. We're remembered for our resilience. Ronald Reagan and Steve Jobs knew that. So did the Midlanders who turned a timber town into a global manufacturing hub, and the Detroiters who have weathered tough times before and will again. As Alan Ott would say, "If you've got lemons, make lemonade."

By learning from the mistakes I've made, embracing the opportunities I've been given and working constantly to improve, I have come to learn that critical lesson myself.

LESSON 4

To Raise Your Game, Listen to Your Coaches

"Do Right: You know what wrong is, so do right."
—Frank Altimore, former Midland Dow High School football coach

The legendary Red Sox hitter Ted Williams supposedly had such incredible eyesight that he could see the stitching on a hanging curveball as it came toward him. He smacked them out of the park, and was the last ballplayer to hit .400. For those in public service, the baseballs are policy issues. They come from the left and from the right. Some are fastballs right over the plate. Others arc slowly and from a great distance. Once in a while, they hit you in the gut. Whatever the case, the key is to see them early, understand their implications for the constituents we serve, and respond quickly and appropriately. Likewise, business leaders need to see the economic curve balls to read the markets quickly and accurately. Jobs, profits and shareholder returns; all these things are at stake.

It sounds like a cliché, but the greatest leaders I've met—not just in politics, but in every occupation—have a well-honed instinct to keep their eye on the ball. They have the ability to see and interpret a broad range of issues, but then to hone in on the critical few that will have the greatest impact.

But while Ted Williams stood alone at the plate waiting for the baseball, most of us rely on others to help us clearly see and address whatever's coming at us—both challenges and opportunities. We need friends and advisors who care enough to be critical, and who are willing to give you a dose of tough love when you need it. We need, in other words, coaches. People who help us train, sharpen and maintain our instincts. People who help us raise our game.

Listen to Your Coach

Clair Bee, a successful college basketball coach as well as the author of the Chip Hilton books I so loved as a kid, once said, "Good coaching may be defined as the development of character, personality and habits of players, plus the teaching of fundamentals and team play." In that sense, I've been fortunate to have a number of great coaches. Some actually held the title "coach"— like Al Quick and Frank Altimore, football coaches at Midland Dow High School, while others were essentially life coaches, before that became a term and a profession.

Coaches can be affirming and uplifting, but they can also be tough. Politics, frankly, doesn't have enough people like that. Let's face it: Politics is full of people who are eager to tell you what you want to hear. The same is true in every other profession. As Spider-Man's Uncle Ben reminds us,

"With great power comes great responsibility." The corollary is that with great power comes a great many people willing to kiss your behind. But as nice as it might be to have everyone simply agree with you regardless of your point, that's seldom, if ever, what's needed. What we really need is not someone who will kiss our behind, but someone who cares enough to kick it from time to time.

Leaders—whether community leaders, elected officials or CEOs—need to find and listen to those critical few trusted counselors who give us tough love and advice when we need it, no matter how difficult it may be to hear.

For me, that person was my stepfather, Carl Gerstacker. Early on, when I was called into his office, it was not for a pat on the back. Most of the time, it was for him to tell me what I was doing wrong or what I should be doing differently. Carl was a brilliant businessman and strategist, and a no-nonsense kind of guy. "Direct" does not begin to describe his style. Without his candid advice and strong support in 1984, I would not have won my congressional race.

But that strong support was not something I could take for granted. Carl was flatly opposed to my decision to run for the U.S. Senate in 1990 and refused to help me in any way. He strongly urged me not to run, said he would not support me and openly discouraged key Dow executives from supporting my campaign. From a career standpoint, this turned out to be sound advice. But at the time, the medicine—and the side effect of his strong, public rejection—was especially painful. I was headstrong and self-assured, and didn't yet appreciate the value of someone so close poking holes, especially after

I announced my candidacy. It took a long time for those wounds to heal between us, and it caused so much stress for my mom during that period.

I contrast that experience with one several years later. Late one Sunday morning, Carl called and asked if he and my mom could come visit us. This was during the almost three years Cynthia and I lived in Lansing, and soon after our daughter Heidi was born. The call was significant because it was a long drive for them—and spontaneous, which wasn't typical. "Uh-oh," I thought. "What have I done wrong this time?"

"I was thinking about you in church this morning," Carl said after they arrived an hour-and-a-half later. "If you want to be in public service and get back in the game, you should run for state Senate. "This is the time," he added, noting that the district lines had just been favorably redrawn. (Given the erosion of our relationship during my U.S. Senate race, Carl's church epiphany was a conversion in every sense of the word.)

At first, I wasn't sure what to do. But again, Carl was giving me sound advice. This time, I was ready to listen and weigh more carefully what he was telling me. Carl's logic and encouragement won me over. Once again, he told me what I needed to hear. And once again, like a good coach, he was right. While I didn't always enjoy the medicine or advice he gave me at the time, in hindsight I know it was always given to be helpful and with my best interests in mind. And this time, he provided me with the boost and tonic I needed to get back in the political ring again.

Of course, there are other ways of giving good advice —less intimidating and authoritative ways. Whatever we do for a living, we all need trusted advisors—formal or informal—who are easy to bounce ideas off of. Any good leader needs frank, sometimes tough, advice, but he or she also needs friends who will listen and provide a safe place to talk through ideas, concerns and options. For me, Alan Ott, Ranny Riecker and Dave Camp—whom I've already mentioned—have fit that bill since I was a child, as does Tom Ludington, now a U.S. federal district judge. There's something special about hometown friends who know you best and have nothing to gain or lose, whether you succeed or fail. They intuitively understand your intentions, passions and doubts. The relationships are honest, the context already understood, and their advice is open, sincere and direct. I always listen carefully, and often follow their advice. Even in the rare times I have gone in a different direction, I've benefited greatly from their perspective.

Jim Barrett, the straight-talking chairman for both of my Attorney General campaigns, is just like that. As the retired president and CEO of the Michigan Chamber of Commerce, he's extremely knowledgeable and a great friend with no ax to grind, and no agenda other than for me to succeed. Talking to Jim always reminds me of Proverbs 20:29 in the Bible, "The glory of young men is their strength, and the splendor of old men is their gray head." Jim's got a lot of experience and a touch of gray, which he draws on to encourage and challenge everyone on the team—especially me. And if, heaven forbid, I start whining about some political situation, Jim's response is as predictable as it is blunt: "Get over it." Good advice.

Another good friend and counselor is Susan Bryant, who was my chief campaign consultant when I ran for the U.S. House of Representatives, the U.S. Senate, the Michigan Senate and the Michigan Court of Appeals. She gave me great, candid advice in so many areas. Some of it was pretty salty. One of my favorite "Susanisms" is, "When you make a mistake, you just have to have a little bite of a s--- sandwich. It doesn't need to be a big bite, just a nibble." And off I would go to apologize or ask for forgiveness, eating what some call "humble pie."

It's not every day that you find a friend who cares about you enough to tell you to take that kind of nibble, but when you find them, don't let them go.

Building a Dream Team

Of course, sometimes the people who will tell it to you straight may not be your best friends. They may be competitors or have their own agendas. But that doesn't mean that their advice can't help you stay focused on what's important.

George H.W. Bush used to say that the mark of leadership was who that leader put on their teams and whose guidance they sought. The best teams include folks whose opinions you value, and who know it's accepted and expected that there will be disagreements and different ideas. You get a better result when you hammer it out first. Once the decision is made, however, everyone on the team should be united.

The foremost example of this is made clear in historian Doris Kearns Goodwin's book, *Team of Rivals: The Political Genius of Abraham Lincoln.* Although William H. Seward, Salmon P. Chase and Edward Bates had all run against Lincoln for the 1860 presidential nomination, Lincoln still saw fit to appoint them as Secretary of State, Secretary of the Treasury and Attorney General, respectively. As he later said, "We needed the strongest men of the party in the Cabinet. We needed to hold our own people together. I had looked the party over and concluded that these were the very strongest men. Then I had no right to deprive the country of their services." (In my current position, I consider Lincoln especially wise for consulting closely with his Attorney General!)

Despite the initial bitterness among them, Lincoln's patience, humor and political genius yielded an outstanding Cabinet that came to respect his outstanding leadership. Having "the very strongest men" offering him unfiltered advice—especially in an unprecedented time of national upheaval—made Lincoln a stronger leader and a better president.

Leaders know that they need others to keep them honest and on track. And they have the confidence to allow divergent opinions and strong wills onto their teams. We should all be so lucky to have the courage to turn competitors into counselors.

Healthy Advice

My stepfather used to say it was crucial to "prune and fertilize." It was his way of explaining the need to continually review and renew his focus on what was most important, and to methodically remove any distractions that could hamper progress in achieving those priorities.

That's how I try to approach my own life and career. It's up to each of us to stay locked in on what's most important. But to do that, it sure helps to surround ourselves with people who aren't afraid to call us out, set us straight and tell us to "get over it" when we risk getting side-tracked.

No matter how old we get or what we seek to do, we all need a good coach.

LESSON 5

Be on Receive, Not Broadcast

"You're short on ears and long on mouth."

—John Wayne

A Yellow Tango

During the 1962 season, New York Mets center fielder Richie Ashburn was having some trouble communicating with the team's new shortstop, Elio Chacón. Ashburn would yell, "I got it!" when running for fly balls, only to have Chacón —a Venezuelan who spoke little English—run into him, not understanding what Ashburn had said. Eventually, Ashburn learned to say, "Yo la tengo!" which is Spanish for "I've got it," so that Chacón would know to back off the play.

In one game, however, Ashburn ran for a ball hit to left-center field shouting, "Yo la tengo!" out of habit. Left fielder Frank Thomas didn't know what he was saying, and the two collided.

As Thomas allegedly asked later, "What the heck is a yellow tango?"

Well, the yellow tango is everywhere. It's on Wall Street and Capitol Hill, in Hollywood, Silicon Valley and any other place you care to name. It's the noise filling our lives, the messages streaming by us like the opening scene in *Star Wars*. In short, it's the most uncoordinated dance in the world, between people opening their mouths and others closing their ears.

Think about it. On an average day, the "Twitterverse" sends more than 140 million tweets. Facebook users update their "statuses" more than 50 million times. CNN plays hour after hour, 24 hours a day. So do FOX, MSNBC, ESPN and countless other stations. In today's overheated media environment, there's constant pressure to be saying something, to live your life out loud and on screen. That's especially true if you're an executive or an elected official, but it's also true of all of us, in both our professional and personal lives.

But if everyone's talking, who's listening? As leaders, we need to stop broadcasting so much and start listening. Because without listening—actively listening—we can't really learn anything. Or as Shakespeare said, "Listen to many, speak to a few." (Not that the Bard of Avon didn't have quite a lot to say.)

Two Ears and One Mouth

The ideal of active listening isn't exactly a new concept. The Greek philosopher Epictetus observed, "We have two ears and one mouth so that we can listen twice as much as we speak." Listening remains just as important nearly 2,000 years later.

But that doesn't mean we've gotten any better at it. According to the business advisor and author Ram Charan, one in four corporate leaders has a listening deficit—which won't shock anyone who's seen their boss going on and on.

Or how often do we run into a friend or colleague, and without breaking stride physically or mentally, have this touching conversation?

"How're you doing?"

"Great. You?"

"Fine, thanks."

And off we go, isolated in our own orbits.

We watched a video at church not long ago that resonated with me. It began with a guy getting in his car and starting his drive to work. Along the way, he keeps getting cut off in traffic and finds himself muttering to himself about the other drivers. As he pulls into a parking lot, another car zips in front of him to get the parking place he was headed toward. Growing increasingly frustrated, he is cut off again, this time by someone who steps in front of him as he walks into a coffee shop near his office. The man looks up and asks God why this is happening to him. As he looks back down and around him, he then realizes all those people who had cut him off or been rude on his commute are now in the coffee shop with him. One wears a sign, "Just Lost His Sister," another says "Just Got Fired." You get the idea.

The fact is, people frequently aren't "fine." They're worried about a sick family member, distracted by an argument with their kids that morning, or perhaps excited about an upcoming vacation. But we'll never know because we often don't really ask—or listen—to the people in our lives. As taught in the Bible, James 1:19, "Let every man be swift to hear, slow to speak, slow to wrath." The message in the video was that we need to take the time to understand, and to be patient and kind to those around us.

In contrast to the automatic pleasantries we typically exchange, Bill Abbatt, a Detroit area attorney and friend, once started a conversation with me by asking, "What did you do today?" It was amazing how that personal question interrupted the typical responses and instead sparked a real conversation—and a real connection.

Part of listening is making ourselves available to others, on their timetable and terms. It takes time, but it's also immensely rewarding. When you actively listen, you affirm that person and cement relationships. I think small towns are better at this, perhaps because we have a lifetime to practice with each other.

I became especially aware of this in my first campaign for Congress. One of the best parts about campaigning, of course, is hearing directly from constituents. Originally, I organized those coffee shop visits I mentioned earlier to increase my visibility throughout the district. But similar to the musical, *A Funny Thing Happened on the Way to the Forum*, it was in those coffee shops, and other similar small venues, where I learned the most—not only about what was happening around town, but what really mattered to people in small towns around our state. When I sat down across the table in their local diner, I could really hear—and come to understand—what peoples' hopes and concerns were. These discussions were the highlights in an otherwise crazy campaign schedule, as they have been in every campaign since.

I also learned to listen from my own campaign team. Bob Stempel, former chairman and CEO of General Motors, was on my U.S. Senate campaign finance committee in 1990. An accomplished business executive, he was also a disciplined listener. During our meetings, he took detailed notes of the discussions and clearly incorporated what he heard into his advice. Perhaps it was his engineering background that made him so disciplined, but it was another lesson in active listening.

Sharing a laugh with former Michigan Attorney General Frank Kelley at the dedication of the Frank J. Kelley Walkway in Lansing, with Governor Rick Snyder, October 2013. (Photo credit: Office of Kelley Cawthorne)

From friends like these and in communities all around Michigan, I learned from and was influenced by people quietly living their small town values. And perhaps most importantly, I learned that if I do a better job listening, and do less talking, I can serve my constituents a whole lot better.

It's a skill we all need to work on in our own offices and homes.

According to Charan, "Despite today's fast-paced business environment, time-starved leaders can master the art of disciplined listening." He suggests a number of tips, including taking notes, understanding the perspective of the source and slowing down long enough to actually absorb the information. Listening well can pay off; GE Chairman and CEO Jeff Immelt, for one, counts "humble listening" as one of the most important traits in a leader.

Likewise, if Cynthia or our children walk into the room as I'm opening the mail, I've learned I need to put down the bills and focus on the conversation. I'm trying, but it's still a work in progress. Same thing with the iPhone—it can wait. Especially when our children became teenagers, I realized how fleeting those moments of real conversation and connection can be. And when they want to talk, whether it's about a major decision or just the day's routine events, I want to fully be there for them. Sometimes the best thing a parent can do, particularly in these whirlwind days, is to just sit back … and listen.

Can You Hear Me Now? Good … and Bad

I'm sure many of us remember those Verizon commercials with an actor traveling the world—from snowy peaks to a bowling alley—asking all the while, "Can you hear me now?

Good!" And those phones, along with all the other hallmarks of our digital age, have indeed made it easier for us to place a call or log in, even if we do decide to surf the web in the middle of the Sahara.

But the irony is that those devices designed to help us be more efficient and connected can also have the opposite effect. Rather than enhancing productivity, they can actually create distractions.

Take just one recent example. Last summer, I attended a big dinner meeting on Mackinac Island, featuring several nationally respected speakers. Looking around the room during the speeches, I was shocked to see a vast majority of the attendees fiddling with their phones. I'm sure some were Tweeting or Facebooking about the event, or maybe even taking notes about what was said. But, really? We ought to be more respectful and attentive to people who are taking the time to share their thoughts with us. Although not always a popular request, I ask my staff to turn off their cell phones when we're meeting.

And then there's that office staple, the speakerphone. It's a great invention—when there are multiple people in a room or if you need both hands to shuffle some documents or take notes. But how often do we hit that button—which, of course, includes that wonderful mute button—and sit back to start checking email? On the other end of the line, you have to wonder: Are they whispering to an unidentified person in the room, flossing their teeth, doing sit-ups? If I suspect I don't have someone's full attention, I may say, "I'm sorry, I can't hear you very well." They usually have to pick up the phone or at least become more fully engaged in the discussion. But the bigger issue is how casually we check out of conversations when we should be more invested.

Tom Hoisington, a great friend and respected lobbyist in Lansing, tells the story of having lunch with a colleague and a political leader in Lansing. He watched as the colleague kept looking at and typing on his phone. "May I borrow your phone?" Tom finally asked. When the friend handed it to him, Tom calmly placed the phone in a glass of water on the table and returned to the conversation. Nothing like drowning out the noise—literally.

Lest I sound too old-fashioned, I should hasten to add that I think technology offers us indispensable tools for doing work and keeping connected, whether we're texting friends and family, streaming our favorite TV show or researching on Wikipedia (I'll admit it, parts of this book have benefitted from the latter). In fact, technology doesn't have to distract us—it can actually make us better communicators. "The digital world that Net Geners have been weaned on is profoundly interactive," said Don Tapscott, the author of *Grown Up Digital.* "Kids have grown up to expect a two-way conversation, not a one-way lecture."

We just have to be disciplined enough to take advantage of those two-way conversations, and make sure we control the constant barrage of texts, tweets and emails we get. We need to make sure we're in the driver's seat, getting the information we need—when and where we need it—and not let the continuous flow of information drive us from our priorities.

At the risk of sounding like John Wayne, "Put down the phone, Pilgrim."

From Listening To Doing:

Acting on What You Hear

During the 1970s, Chrysler fell on tough times. The company was disorganized and on the verge of bankruptcy. After recalls of the Dodge Aspen and Plymouth Volare, brand loyalty was dangerously low. The 1973 oil shock and a deep recession didn't help.

Enter Lee Iacocca, previously the president of Ford Motor Company.

Iacocca took a number of dramatic actions to rescue Chrysler, including laying off 33 of 35 vice presidents, closing plants and selling off entire divisions of the company. But one of his most significant changes was a simple one – he listened. As longtime Chrysler employee Bill Wetherholt recalls, "Iacocca said that the workers have a lot to offer, so you should listen to the workers. We started forming these group meetings, product quality meetings, and you would mark down things that would make your job better, and they came in with ergonomics and things like that. Iacocca ... wanted to change the way we operated."

As Iacocca himself would say, "I only wish I could find an institute that teaches people how to listen. Business people need to listen at least as much as they need to talk.

Too many people fail to realize that real communication goes in both directions." In his estimation, "Listening can make the difference between a mediocre company and a great company."

If active listening is really about learning, then accurately understanding what we hear leads to accurate actions. It's all too easy to jump to the wrong conclusions and then respond too quickly or in error. Like Richie Ashburn yelling in Spanish to the wrong teammate, we need to make sure we're fully listening to what's being said—and sometimes even what isn't being said—whether it's coming from shareholders, constituents or family members.

In October 2010, for instance, former Florida Governor Jeb Bush spoke at a large fundraising dinner in Metro Detroit for Yeshiva Beth Yehudah, a large, 100-year-old Jewish school system, just a few weeks prior to Election Day and with my opponent in the audience as well. During the dinner, Bush got up to give his speech … and didn't mention me at all. I was a bit hurt and frustrated because we knew each other well and I had worked on several Bush family campaigns. Luckily, I did not react or voice my frustration during the dinner. I learned later that Jeb had been asked not to mention specific candidates or discuss state political issues during his formal remarks. At a private reception of the leaders following the dinner, however, I heard he was very positive and offered several kind comments about me.

It was an important lesson that we need to listen and understand the context before drawing conclusions. I wrote a note to Jeb after the event, not only to thank him for attending the fundraiser and for his support, but also to share what I had learned in the process.

Another one of Al Ott's gems speaks to this point—this time he gave me advice on getting advice. His admonition was straightforward: If you ask for someone's advice, be prepared to take it. If you don't follow their advice after you've asked for it, you risk alienating or offending them, and they're not likely to invest the time in the future, either. Similar to my education as an attorney, I've learned over the years to only ask questions when I am prepared to hear the answer. I might ask others for their opinion or perspective, but asking someone for advice means not only listening to the answer, but being prepared to act on it.

As the actor Alan Alda reminds us, "Listening is being able to be changed by the other person."

And with that, I'll stop broadcasting.

Attending a 2014 fundraiser for Governor Rick Snyder's re-election campaign in Grand Rapids (l to r): former Florida Governor Jeb Bush, me, Michigan Governor Rick Snyder and former Michigan Governor John Engler. (Photo credit: Jim Hill Photography)

LESSON 6

Leadership Is Hands-On

"He didn't just tell us how something should be done. He showed us. Coach Wooden was right out there on the court with us demonstrating even though he must have been 40 years older than us. This means something — to see him out there doing it himself."

— Kareem Abdul-Jabbar, describing UCLA Coach John Wooden

Make Your Own Phone Calls

During the George W. Bush administration, comedian Jon Stewart liked to imagine Vice President Dick Cheney speaking with Darth Vader's menacing voice. But the truth is, Dick Cheney is a fine man and a lot more personable than he's given credit for—and he doesn't sound like Darth at all. I can say that with certainty because one day, Cheney called my state Senate office. That's right—the vice president of the United States called a state senator. Personally. I was under consideration for an ambassadorship at the time, and Cheney himself placed the call to discuss it with me.

Our office intern just about swallowed his tongue when he answered the phone, because the vice president of the United States, not an assistant, was on the line. Here was Cheney, arguably one of the most active and influential VPs in history, and yet he had mastered a lesson my stepfather also taught: "Always make your own phone calls."

It may seem like a small thing, but it's actually a perfect illustration of the virtues of engaged, hands-on leadership —and one of the most valuable lessons I've learned. Good leaders pay attention to even the smallest details, taking note of when someone might appreciate a personal call.

At the same time, I've come to understand that good leaders cannot endlessly micromanage. You have to delegate routine work and trust, and empower your team to act on their own. In other words, strong leaders have to be both hands-on and hands-off. It's a tough balance to strike, but the leaders who manage it are able, simultaneously, to be engaged with their organizations and free to focus on the big picture.

Building Relationships with Your Team

My father, William H. Schuette, was well-respected and liked at The Dow Chemical Company, where he worked. Whether he was visiting the manufacturing floor or in the boardroom, he was the same down-to-earth person, equally interested in the work and the people. I was just six years old when he passed away, but over the years I've heard countless stories from family, friends and former employees, all sharing how "normal" he was, how easy to talk to. Although I had far too few years to personally learn from him, my dad has been a lifelong role model and continues to be my inspiration as a father and a leader.

Congressman Dick Cheney and me in a discussion at a Republican Policy Conference in 1986. (Photo credit: Bill Schuette)

I had more time to learn from my stepfather, Carl. During my first political campaign, he encouraged me to invest significant time with people—not just prospective voters, but paid staff and volunteers as well. I quickly saw the benefits of his advice. When people give their time and energy to help your campaign—or even just to learn about your candidacy and what you believe in—they deserve more than a wave or a handshake. If you take the time to learn about a colleague's motivations or characteristics—are they night owls or morning people; do they have an ailing parent to care for—you're better able to understand and work with the people around you. And, you're more likely to earn their respect.

I also had this lesson brought home to me, thanks to a business executive from Midland, Keith McKennon. Although I didn't have the good fortune of working for him, I could see that Keith was the best kind of hands-on leader. He had an easy smile, a quick wit and a brilliant mind. Everyone respected him as a remarkable listener and counselor throughout his career at Dow, and later as CEO of Dow Corning. In my 1990 U.S. Senate race, during the time my stepfather and I were estranged, Keith stepped in to help fill the gap. In the evenings, we'd sit on his back porch and talk about the race, but also about life in general.

Keith made time for this even though he had a big job at Dow, and even though he was undergoing aggressive cancer treatments and had three sons and his wife to think about. Still, he sat with me and helped me navigate my personal and political crises. Sadly, Keith died of cardiac arrest in September 2013, the first and only time in his life that his heart failed him.

Great leaders get personally engaged. Whether it's in the boardroom or on the playing field, they not only understand interpersonal dynamics, they see human beings as human beings and understand, or at least work hard to understand, their motivations and challenges.

Great leaders are hands-on within their organizations. They want to know not only who's doing a good job and who isn't, but also whose kid is having a great Little League season or who is celebrating a birthday or anniversary. We need to be sincerely interested in each other and the day-to-day activities that comprise our lives. Only by understanding the full person, and by connecting personally, can a leader truly and effectively lead.

You Can't Just "Wing It"

Another crucial part of hands-on leadership lies in careful —almost obsessive—preparation. Like the old Boy Scout and Girl Scout mottos, leaders must "Be prepared." (Picking up the Scout slogan, "Do a good turn daily," wouldn't hurt either.) Throughout my career, I've seen this drive to be thoroughly prepared in political and business leaders alike.

In the days leading up to national elections there always is a flurry of activity and 1984 was no exception. I was in full campaign mode but was down in the polls 8-10 points just four days prior to the election and the outcome of the race looked bleak. Thankfully, help was on the way. Just like when Iron Man comes to the rescue in an *Avengers* movie, my friend Jim Baker was on his way.

Baker was managing Ronald Reagan's re-election campaign. He had arranged for the president to make a critical stop at our airport on the Friday prior to the Tuesday election, to help push me over the top in my congressional race. I met up with him at the Renaissance Center in Detroit and together we headed to the basement, where he told me to hop into one of the black limos idling in the garage. As

I jumped into the car, I bumped into someone in the back seat. Turning to apologize, I found myself face-to-face with the Leader of the Free World. Fortunately, President Reagan didn't seem to mind.

In fact, he was quietly working on his speech note cards. I watched him write down "shoe" and "tee" on one of the cards, to make sure he pronounced my last name correctly. I remember thinking to myself, *"Here's the President of the United States, with so many issues demanding his attention, and he's still focused on minor details like pronouncing a candidate's name right."*

President Ronald Reagan makes a last-minute campaign stop near Midland in 1984, helping me come from behind to win election to the U.S. House of Representatives. (Photo credit: Midland Daily News)

President Ronald Reagan speaking at MBS airport in November 1984, days prior to the national election. (Photo credit: Midland Daily News)

Likewise, Richard DeVos, one of the founders of Amway, once invited me to attend a large distributor meeting when I was running for office. He is an outstanding communicator and can hold huge audiences spellbound, which is why I was fascinated to see he had a tiny slip of paper, dwarfed by his hand that I could see from my vantage onstage. I again was impressed that even such a gifted and experienced orator would have such discipline and preparation. Both Reagan and DeVos are known as accomplished speakers and leaders, yet they never took it for granted or stopped preparing for the next speech, the next event. I guess you don't get to be the Great Communicator without paying attention to those kinds of details.

Baker exhibited this same discipline during the period when I worked for him on the Gerald Ford presidential campaign. In one meeting, we were counting delegates state-by-state and someone suggested to him that we should enter the data into a computer. Jim smiled, pointed to his head, and said, "I don't need a computer; it's all right here." To this day, I don't think they've invented a microchip that could compete with a mind like Jim's.

Another time, Jim was called away from a meeting with someone who was complaining about something or other. He called me into the office where they were meeting and told me to write down everything the man said. "Everything," he said. "I want to read it when I come back." So I did, though it wasn't until later that I also appreciated the importance of that visitor knowing that what he said—specifically and in detail—was important and would be heard.

I've also learned about preparation from our daughter, Heidi. She has always been very organized so it was no surprise that she was equally disciplined in her post-college job search. A college senior, she organized job interviews for Fridays when she didn't have class. As I was driving around the state campaigning for the Attorney General position in the fall of 2014, Heidi would schedule practice interviews with me before each interview. And not surprisingly, her hard work has paid off. She landed a great job following graduation.

The Little Things That Aren't So Little

We've all heard the proverbial mother's lament to her child: "You never call, you never write!" Most of us neglect to do either, even as adults. Yet the personal effort of calling or hand-writing a note sends a profound message to the recipient that they are important to you.

One of my biggest pet peeves is when "important people" forget my stepfather's long-ago lesson and have someone call on their behalf. "Hello, this is Jack Smith, please hold while I connect you with Sue Jones." It's disrespectful in so many ways, from the implied superiority of the caller to the time that is wasted while connections are made. Like that Cheney phone call, the best leaders, in my experience, make their own calls. When my stepfather Carl Gerstacker died in 1995, for instance, President Gerald Ford called our house three times until he could reach me personally to express his condolences. And I remember that kindness. You honor the recipient when you personally call or write.

I've seen the flip side of returning calls, as well. When you're in a position of influence, it's amazing who calls— and how quickly your calls are returned. But as soon as that position is taken away, by a vote of the electorate or a board of directors, the phone line might as well be dead. Many of those who clamored to speak with you when you were "important" not only don't call, they don't return your calls.

When this happened to me, it took a while to learn not to take it personally. Our work lives are filled with transactional

President Gerald R. Ford helping my name recognition by displaying a campaign T-shirt during my 1984 race for the U.S. House of Representatives. (Photo credit: Bill Schuette)

relationships based on the position we hold or the work that we do. But having been on the receiving end of this experience has taught me how meaningful it is always to respect individuals, regardless of their position, and always to return personal calls.

Shortly after I was elected to the Michigan Court of Appeals, I had to adjust to the new title of "Judge." It's kind of like buying a new pair of shoes; they feel a bit stiff until you use them for a while. I needed to call someone in my official capacity, and explained to the assistant who answered that I was Judge Schuette. The person I was calling appeared on the line like greased lightning and seemed a little out of breath—like he was excited about something. I said "Hello, this is Bill Schuette," and asked how he was doing. There was a long pause. Then he responded, much more subdued, "Oh, hi, Bill. My assistant told me *Judge Judy* was on the line."

I continued, after that, to place my own phone calls. I just make sure to pronounce my name a little more clearly. Although from time to time, if I'm concerned about getting through to someone, it's tempting to mumble just a little bit.

A Note on Thank-You Notes

For those who think a quick e-mail is good enough to connect with someone, here's a quick note on thank-you notes.

Ranny Riecker taught me the importance of thank-you notes early. I would wander into her house after mowing the lawn, and often find her, in her role as National Republican Committeewoman for Michigan, personally writing and signing stacks of letters. Ranny taught me the importance of personalizing letters—of crossing out the "Mr." and "Mrs." and handwriting the first names, and adding a personal note and signature at the bottom. I still do that to this day.

Likewise, the Bush family has an amazing reputation for writing personal notes, making personal calls and most important, maintaining close relationships with friends and former colleagues and staff. In 2000, George H.W. Bush published *All the Best, George Bush: My Life in Letters and Other*

Writings. In a sense, you could call this a memoir, because his public life is contained in those handwritten letters.

It really got rolling when Bush was a congressman, back in the 1960s. A woman from Houston wrote him a letter, so Congressman Bush wrote back. She replied, thanking him for the note, so Congressman Bush wrote her back again, thanking her for the thank-you note … and so on. That's the kind of man he is. After an event, the first thing he'd do was ask for the list of attendees, and start penning thank-you notes—on the plane, in his study and at all hours of the day. Over the years, Barbara Bush accumulated a massive file of some 5,000 cards, each one neatly filled out with the names and updated addresses of friends who would be sent those notes.

I've kept every note he wrote to me and I'm sure most others have done the same. I received my very first note from him in 1979 after I, a young campaign volunteer, had picked him up at the Grand Rapids airport in my mother's Jeep. We stayed at what was then the Holiday Inn on Ann Street. (Those were the good old days when a presidential candidate could travel casually.) On the front of the card, outlined in blue, was the name George Bush. Gratitude—genuine gratitude—goes a long way and like most recipients, I've never forgotten that personal touch.

In fact, I ordered personalized note cards that looked a lot like his, and still use them to regularly hand write notes today. I've also kept a note his mother, Dorothy Walker Bush, sent me after the 1979 Florida primary, which her son George H.W. had lost to Ronald Reagan. (I was Bush's Florida campaign

GEORGE BUSH
710 NORTH POST OAK ROAD
SUITE 208
HOUSTON, TEXAS 77024
(713) 467-1980

9.22-79

Dear Bill -
You are doing a first
class job and I am really
grateful. Keep it up!
we will find a good
chairmen. Loret Ruppe
will help us + think about

it - so will the Gov.
I may get Jim Baker
to fly up to see Romney.
May my thanks,
Geo B

One of my first thank-you notes from George H. W. Bush, which he sent after I had driven him around Michigan in my mother's Jeep. (Credit: Bill Schuette)

P. O. BOX 551
HOBE SOUND, FLORIDA 33455

Dear Bill -
            Thanks for your
note, Florida was a great
disappointment & George says
he has no hopes for Illinois
to-day - but next week
he may be able to start answer

up hill all the way
Barry so last his physical
strength gives out
He is by far the best
candidate - Why can't
all the Reps. in the country
see that - Yours Sincerely,
            Dorothy W. Bush

I met Dorothy Walker Bush, George H.W. Bush's mother, at her Florida home in 1979 and sent a note afterwards thanking her for her hospitality. In classic Bush family tradition, she sent this thank-you note in return. (Credit: Bill Schuette)

manager.) Obviously, Bush had learned an important lesson from his mother.

Leading an Organization

That said, a hands-on leader must also know when and how to be hands-off.

By the time he was 42, Theodore Roosevelt had written highly respected works of history and botany, charged San Juan Hill in Cuba, tracked down and captured three outlaws in the Dakota badlands, and served as New York State Assemblyman, U.S. Civil Service commissioner, New York police commissioner, assistant secretary of the U.S. Navy, colonel of the 1st U.S. Volunteer Cavalry (the "Rough Riders"), governor of New York, vice president of the United States, and president of the United States. The man was probably the most active and hands-on executive in the history of the U.S.—if not the history of the planet.

So it might come as a surprise that the Rough Rider was also a delegator. But he was, and enthusiastically so. As Roosevelt himself once said, "The best executive is the one who has sense enough to pick good men to do what he wants done, and self-restraint to keep from meddling with them while they do it."

It's a good motto and a lesson for us all. The Michigan Attorney General's office is engaged in more than 40,000 cases each year. Naturally, I'm unable to directly work on every aspect of every case myself, so I invest significant time with the organization and our key personnel to ensure that the decisions made are aligned with what I would do, and that every case is handled professionally and consistently.

Celebrating Peter and Joan Secchia's 50th Wedding Anniversary in Grand Rapids in June 2014 (l to r): MSU Athletic Director Mark Hollis and his wife Nancy, MSU Head Football Coach Mark Dantonio and his wife Becky, and Cynthia and me. (Photo credit: Jim Hill Photography)

Michigan was host to the 2014 National Association of Attorneys General, and several Michigan leaders spoke to the group, including Mark Dantonio, Michigan State University's head football coach. A 34-year collegiate coach with 19 bowl game appearances, Mark said his job is to motivate and inspire his team, listen, encourage, mentor, teach—and delegate. As

I listened to him, I was struck by how much we need to adopt these attributes as leaders wherever we are.

Michigan is fortunate to have outstanding legal professionals in the Attorney General's office, so my focus is on cultivating an environment that allows them—and all of us—to succeed. That begins with a culture that is open, direct, prompt, respectful and always, always committed to producing high-quality work. When issues or problems arise—and as in any organization, they do—we focus first on solving it, then on learning from the situation. This philosophy was tested in March 2015, when our office wrongly issued subpoenas to reporters interviewing prison inmates regarding a lawsuit claiming sexual abuse by prison guards. I apologized to the two reporters, and took responsibility on behalf of our office.

I've seen the chilling effect in an organization when leaders hover over and only criticize or second-guess their staff. Instead, we try to promote a positive, problem-solving atmosphere. As Henry Ford liked to say, "Don't find fault; find a remedy."

And, I would add, find the balance between engagement and delegation—hands-on leadership that isn't, well, heavy-handed.

Be the Real Deal

"To be yourself in a world that is constantly trying to make you something else is the greatest accomplishment."

— Ralph Waldo Emerson

"You Can't Plant 10 Rows of Corn with a 12-Row Planter"

Gratiot County is in the middle of the state, and has some of the best farmland in Michigan. Over the years, I have spent a lot of time in Gratiot and rural areas like it —learning about dairy operations, visiting hog farms and walking through row crops. Along the way I met and became friends with Rex and Kathy Crumbaugh, who lived in the small town of Breckenridge, up in the northeast corner of the county. They farmed their 3,500 acre family operation, and explained to me the issues and concerns they and their neighbors faced.

I knew zero about farming, but they taught me so much, including the unique business challenges and important role agriculture has in our region. Rex and Kathy also showed me their operation, the highlight of which was climbing into the cab of a big John Deere tractor with Rex one morning and riding along as he planted corn.

That evening, I spoke at a community dinner and enthusiastically described my day. "Today, thanks to Rex, I planted my first 10 rows of corn, which was just terrific," I told the audience. Later, Kathy and Rex pulled me aside, their eyes twinkling with laughter. "You know, Bill, you're a hard worker and you're going to be a good voice for agriculture," they said. "But we just wanted you to know... you really can't plant 10 rows of corn with a 12-row planter."

Oops.

I may have turned red as a barn that evening, but I'll never forget the lesson that Rex and Kathy taught me: One day on a farm does not a farmer make. I could and did, however, learn what was important to our region's farmers, which helped me become a better advocate for them when I later served on the House Agriculture Committee. Rex passed away not too long ago; I miss him and will never forget his kindness.

Cynthia and me at the Michigan State Fair in 1991. We had just finished competing in the cow-milking contest, in which Cynthia won a ribbon (for the record, I didn't). (Photo credit: Bill Schuette)

Another time during the same campaign, I was able to humorously embrace my lack of farming bona fides while remaining true to who I really was. Congressman Don Albosta, my opponent, had been a farmer; I clearly had not grown up in a farming family. We argued fiercely over who would best represent farmers. At one point, Albosta made some snide remarks that my only agricultural knowledge came from our family's gardeners. With a healthy pinch of salt, my campaign made up buttons that said "Gardeners for Schuette." And those wonderful farmers in mid-Michigan?

Sure enough, they appreciated the joke—and the point. And they had fun wearing them.

We made "Gardeners for Schuette" buttons after my opponent said my only knowledge of farming came from the family's gardeners. The agricultural community enjoyed the humor, and wore the pins, too. (Credit: Bill Schuette)

It's like Jerry Lewis, the comedian who would laugh, sing, dance and cry his way through the 24-hour Labor Day

Muscular Dystrophy Telethon. For half a century, Lewis was a tireless advocate, raising nearly $2 billion for muscular dystrophy research and serving as the association's national chairman for 55 years. But he never pretended to be the expert. He understood that his role was to bring the cause to the public, and he found a way into the hearts of millions of viewers—and ultimately, donors—across the country.

As a public servant, the role is much the same. We champion public policy on behalf of our constituents, bringing visibility to and, hopefully, support for the issues that matter to them. Obviously, it's important to become as informed as possible on subjects your constituents care about. But the key to good advocacy, whether you're on the local school board or a nationally elected figure, is to find and listen carefully to the real experts on an issue—folks like Kathy and Rex – and then spend more time posing questions than posing for photo ops.

In a world of fake smiles, I've learned that you've got to avoid what's artificial and reach for the real. No matter where you are or where you're from, whether you're evaluating political candidates or just trying to be the best person you can be, authenticity is the coin of the realm. It's rare to find someone who is "the real deal," but that's exactly what we should all strive to be. It may be a "corny" lesson, but it's the truth.

Stay True to Yourself

There are a whole lot of perks to being elected president of the United States. You have Air Force One at your command,

and might meet with Warren Buffett and golf with Tiger Woods all on the same day. Your childhood idols can't wait to take your calls. And if you're "President George H.W. Bush" —well, you finally don't have to eat broccoli.

Bush famously declared in 1990, "I do not like broccoli. And I haven't liked it since I was a little kid and my mother made me eat it. And I'm president of the United States and I'm not going to eat any more broccoli."

For me, it's dress shoes with laces. When I was running in 1984, my advisers told me to wear them to make me look older and more mature, so I did. I hated those shoes. And I threw them out the day after the election. And it's not often that I've worn dress shoes with laces since.

An early campaign challenge was to help people pronounce my name. The "shoe-T" prop, created by my political expert (Mom!), worked well and was one of few good uses for my dress shoes with shoelaces. (Photo credit: Bill Schuette)

The point is, it can be a challenge for people in public roles to stay true to themselves. Even Bush's simple statement of his culinary preferences launched a storm of protests, with farmers sending truckloads of broccoli to the White House in protest.

In politics, with so many consultants and handlers telling you which poll-tested message to say or where to grab a sandwich, it's easy to become a cardboard cut-out, a prop who shakes hands, kisses babies and praises the American flag. With endless photo ops and sound bites, there's constant pressure to stay on message. To have a comment on every situation, no matter how well- or ill-informed you may be. And if you're not very careful, you can easily lose sight of who you really are.

Gary Hart, the senator from Colorado, twice ran for president, in 1984 and 1988. Both times, he damaged his prospects because the voters questioned his authenticity. It wasn't only his extramarital affairs, which the press pursued mercilessly. It was also the way he reportedly imitated John and Robert Kennedy too closely, that he'd changed his name and that he'd misstated his age at one point.

In contrast, it's refreshing to see very public people who consciously and confidently remain centered, attuned to who they are and what their priorities are. Pope Francis, for instance, is such a person. Born Jorge Bergoglio, he took Francis as his papal name in honor of St. Francis of Assisi, a saint devoted to humility and the poor. But far from confining his focus on the poor to that single symbolic act, he has truly walked the walk. Pope Francis dresses simply and traded in the glass-enclosed "Popemobile" for a used 1984 Renault. He celebrated his birthday meal with the homeless and has washed the feet of criminals. He lives in a Vatican residence along with clergy and lay people rather than the lavish papal quarters. "I'm visible to people and I lead a normal life—a public Mass in the morning, I eat in the refectory with everyone else, et cetera," Pope Francis wrote to Father Enrique Martinez. "All this is good for me and prevents me from being isolated."

Find Your Way Home

If the Pope can stay that down-to-earth, the rest of us certainly should be able to stay true to ourselves. Still, leading the hectic lives we do, it can be a challenge to carve out time to just be "normal." Long-time House Republican Leader Bob Michel used to say he wanted to return home to Peoria, Illinois and work in his garden. I get that, because that's my way of relaxing too. I'm a whole lot happier if I can stop by the Ace Hardware store down on Main Street, pick up some yard supplies and then head home to work in the yard. I think the joy of working outside goes back to my fond memories of Ranny and John Riecker. To this day, nothing relaxes or grounds me more than working in our yard at home (though I steer clear of the 12-row planters).

Going home gives me a chance to reset my compass, recharge my batteries and reinforce those small town values. After a long day or week, it's nice to pull into our driveway in Midland. Over the weekend, I might pop into the local grocery store, run into people who have known me or my family for years, talk about the price of gas or about the local high school sports teams. And when I'm unwinding at home, you might find me in my stocking feet, or perhaps in tennis shoes or loafers, but never, ever in dress shoes with laces.

LESSON 8

Give and Let Give

"I must say that I have seen Americans make a great deal of real sacrifices to the public welfare; and have noticed a hundred instances in which they hardly ever failed to lend a faithful support to one another."

— Alexis de Tocqueville

When I was home for a weekend break from college, Saturdays were for football or goofing around. That is, until I received my formal introduction to philanthropy— to the importance and discipline of giving—in 1975 when I was a college senior. A Saturday in December, just before Christmas, meant it was time for a board meeting of the Rollin M. Gerstacker Foundation in our dining room.

The Gerstacker Foundation was founded by my stepfather's mother to assure that the charities she and her husband Rollin supported would continue to flourish after she died. Originally, these meetings were on Saturdays to avoid interfering with the work week, though I'm happy to report that the meetings are now during the work week, giving members back their Saturday afternoons. My stepsister, Lisa, remains dedicated to our family foundation, serving as president.

Early on, I saw and learned that successful organizations and individuals can't just take from a community and expect to thrive. You have to support the community that supports you.

The dedicated Board of Trustees of the Rollin M. Gerstacker Foundation, 2012. Members included front row (l to r): E. N. Brandt, Lisa Gerstacker, Gail Allen Lanphear, me, and Alan Ott. 2nd row: Ruth Ann Wright (administrative assistant), William S. Stavropoulos, Paula Liveris, Paul F. Oreffice, Alexio Baum, Thomas Ludington and Frank Gerace. (Photo credit: Rollin M. Gerstacker Foundation)

Those who did well living and working in our small town felt a responsibility to invest some of their earnings in a brighter future for those who would follow. People "paid it forward," donating to worthy civic causes, from medicine to education to the arts.

As with many of the lessons we learn, my mother and stepfather probably taught Lisa and me the most about philanthropy. My stepfather's strong sense of pride in and responsibility to Midland defined him, especially after he retired. He believed that the institutions that mattered should be maintained and improved for the long haul. While they contributed to many different organizations, my parents practiced a particularly local form of philanthropy. Like many of Midland's early civic leaders, they believed they could make the biggest positive difference in the lives of their own neighbors.

Watching my mother and Carl engage in the civic life of Midland—funding senior centers and bridges, endowing scholarships, beautifying the community—I came to understand the importance of using private funds for public ends. Our means may vary, but the desire and ability to contribute should be—and is—within the reach of us all. It's something we can teach our young people, and hopefully foster throughout our lives.

Leave Your Campsite Better

Than You Found It

When I was young, I was taught to leave a campsite cleaner than I found it, and this same philosophy applies to the organizations to which we belong or support. It's true for our houses of worship—churches, synagogues and mosques. It's true for educational and medical programs, as well as civic and youth organizations. Everywhere we look, we see evidence of these big-hearted efforts to enhance the world around us.

If you look around Michigan, for example, you'll notice one fairly prominent name—Frederik Meijer. For a lot of people, Meijer's name is the one dotting more than 200 supermarkets throughout Michigan and the Midwest. But that's not the only place you'll see his contributions. The Frederik Meijer Gardens & Sculpture Park near Grand Rapids features more than 300 sculptures, with pieces from Alexander Calder to Claes Oldenburg. It is the second most-popular tourist attraction in Michigan and among the 100 most-visited art museums in the world, drawing more than half a million visitors annually.

Meijer, his wife Lena, and their sons have given millions to charitable causes, ranging from public parks to a public broadcasting center. Patients receive world-class treatment at the Meijer Heart Center; students participate in the Meijer Good Schools for Grand Rapids Program and earn Meijer Scholarships; patrons of the arts enjoy performances at the

Meijer Majestic Theatre; and hikers stride along the many miles of the Meijer Midwest Michigan Trail Authority Network.

According to Larry ten Harmsel, who co-authored *Fred Meijer: Stories of His Life*," Meijer said, "You know, spending this money is almost as much fun as making it. I've had so much in my life, I hope other people can have that and live as long." In a lot of respects, Meijer didn't just leave the campsite better than he found it; he built the campsite from scratch, enhanced it in a hundred inspiring and enduring ways, and only then left it to the next generation. His generous example is one that I strive to emulate. Philanthropically speaking, West Michigan is blessed with many generous families, such as the DeVos, Murray, Secchia, and Van Andel families, as well as many others.

Often, community philanthropy takes the form not just of financial contributions, but time and strategic investments, as well. Take Jim Nicholson, president and CEO of the Detroit-based PVS Chemicals, Inc. Even when others abandoned Detroit for other cities or states, Jim and his family have continued investing in the city. Jim's contributions have involved spending hours of his time steering and advising civic organizations. His civic leadership is so extensive that Jim's the rare person who can say he's not only been honored by both the YMCA and the American Jewish Federation but in 2004, also was named Michiganian of the Year. His family's contributions have had a tremendous positive impact on southeast Michigan and the state overall.

Southeast Michigan also has a history of generous philanthropic roots, from the late Max Fisher and Al Taubman, to current giants Roger Penske and Dan Gilbert and leaders Dave Fischer, Peter Karmanos, John Rakolta, Jr., Bobby Schostak, Ron Weiser and Bill Young.

While Grand Rapids and Detroit can't exactly be considered small towns—except maybe in comparison to Tokyo or New York City—there are many who demonstrate the tremendous impact we can all have when we give back to and invest in the future of the places and programs important to us.

Helping To Fill a Need, However You Can

Being generous and making contributions is much more about the mindset of the individual than the balance in their bank account. In fact, one study calculates that those making between $25,000 to $30,000 a year give away more on a percentage basis than wealthier families—4.2 percent of their income compared to 2.7 percent. Beyond financial contributions, however, there is so much we can all give. For example, we can volunteer our time and expertise. We can mentor and tutor, or become Big Brothers and Big Sisters. Growing up, we never had a shortage of coaches or volunteer librarians because everyone understood that there was always a way to give back. Hokey as it sounds, I truly believe that what matters is not what's in your bank account, but what's in your heart.

When it came time to build the unique three-spoke bridge that spans the Chippewa and Tittabawassee Rivers in Midland, it wasn't just a project for the town's leading citizens and philanthropists. Kids in the community pitched in, as well, pennies at a time. As my mother wrote about the project, "With the help of the Midland Area Community Foundation, the community raised the matching money and children carried in hundreds of bags of pennies to the bank, even naming the Tridge and writing a song. The whole community united to make this Tridge possible; it's something I will never forget."

In Midland, we have been blessed with marvelous corporate leaders who make big investments to build a stronger town. Paul F. Oreffice, former CEO and Chairman of Dow, a family friend and a Gerstacker Foundation trustee, made a huge impact by spearheading the construction of Midland's expansive soccer complex and the development of world-class courts at the Midland Community Tennis Center.

The trick to philanthropy is to match the personal interests and experiences of the donors with the needs of others. Philanthropist Peter Lynch is often quoted for his advice to only "buy what you know," and the natural corollary of that is that each of us should focus our philanthropy on the organizations we know well and the issues we care about most. Our contributions—financial or otherwise—should fill a need, and that need should be one we see and feel most acutely in our lives. At least, that's how I've tried to act.

As Heidi was getting ready to start kindergarten, I remember Cynthia and me visiting Carpenter Street Elementary School, with Heidi and toddler Bill in tow. It was the first time we'd been inside since we were students ourselves; your children attending the same elementary school is one of the hallmarks of small-town living. The windows had been bricked over during the energy crisis of the 1970s, leaving very little natural light inside the building. We talked with friends and local foundations, and a fundraising effort was started to restore the windows. Together, friends and alumni of the little elementary school raised the needed money and, after a few carpenters descended on Carpenter Street, the school became a lot lighter and brighter for the students—and looks a lot nicer outside too. I'm not sure the group would have felt the same urgency if we hadn't known the school and its history so intimately.

Cynthia and I were similarly concerned by the situation we saw back in 1991, when Michigan faced nine percent unemployment and demonstrators built a tent city across from the Capitol in Lansing to protest pending welfare cuts. The Department of Agriculture, where I worked at the time, faced similar budget constraints despite the expanded needs in the state. People were struggling. Expressing my frustration to Cynthia after work one night, she started exploring potential solutions and suggested we do something personally to help. It was her inspiration that got us started.

After some research, we decided to help Michigan's food banks. They were—and are—very well-run nonprofit organizations with low administrative costs, which meant that donations were used efficiently to get food to people in need. Cynthia and I launched the Michigan Harvest Gathering in 1991, an annual fundraising campaign that raises food and funds for the Food Bank Council of Michigan. Since then, as I've said earlier, the campaign has produced more than 9.5 million pounds of food and raised more than $9.3 million for Michigan families. Of all the projects that we've worked on, this simple campaign and its direct support to people in need has been the most gratifying to us as a family. It's also been a good reminder that when times are tough and government budgets are tight, private philanthropy plays a critical role in caring for our most vulnerable.

More importantly, this lesson about "give and let give" is that we give generously and with an open heart.

LESSON 9
Cultivate Your Community

"No man is an island, entire of itself; every man is a
piece of the continent, a part of the main."
–John Donne

The View from the Tridge

In the middle of Midland, as I've mentioned, there's a bridge. It's a wooden footbridge—a unique one—with three branches radiating out from a central column. They've got a small one like it in Ypsilanti, Michigan, and a massive three-way bridge in China, but ours was built before all of those, in 1981. We call our tri-bridge "the Tridge," and a lot of community events in Midland swirl across and around it, from the annual Riverdays event in the summer to the Tridge Walk on Labor Day to Santa's highly anticipated arrival in December.

Every Wednesday and Saturday, from May through October, the Midland Area Farmers Market next to the Tridge bustles with activity. Young and old bike, walk and run on the Pere Marquette Rail Trail nearby. People walk dogs and toss Frisbees. Teenagers pass through on their way to play softball, and at night you see families, couples and groups of friends walk under the bridge's lighted arches on their way to grab pizza or ice cream at Pizza Sam's on Main Street. On nice days, you can find a fisherman who has dropped a line, hoping to catch a walleye at the confluence of the Chippewa and Tittabawassee Rivers. Local bands play concerts during the summer, ranging from bluegrass to jazz.

The Tridge is especially meaningful to me because my mom and Carl helped build it. In fact, they helped to start the community foundation, now called the Midland Area Community Foundation (MACF), which proposed the project and spearheaded the fundraising. It was built, as I've said, not just for the community, but by the community with the pennies of children and the contributions of many Midlanders.

According to the MACF, in the more than 30 years since, "The Tridge has been a gem of our community, a gathering place, an icon, and truly a symbol of our ingenuity and willingness to work together." It's solid, well-used and a testament to hard work. The structure practically radiates small town values and big-hearted civic responsibility.

It just goes to show that when you're from a place like Midland, people don't just live next to each other, they live with each other. These days, it may seem like we're all fixated on the "I" in our iPhones. And yet, I grew up—and still live—in a town where there's a strong emphasis on "we." That experience has convinced me that we need to be alert to the people around us, and make an extra effort to support and encourage one other. Because community is not a given. It's something we build—together.

The Tridge, Midland's three-legged bridge, is a community treasure built in 1981 with funds donated by school children and the community. (Photo credit: R. Scott Williams, Getty Images)

Carl and Esther Gerstacker, my step-father and mother. (Photo credit: Rollin M. Gerstacker Foundation)

The Importance of Cultivating Community

Nowadays, cultivating community is not always easy. When I was a kid, people tended to be defined by community and kin. You'd describe someone in relation to their family: "Matt is one of the Thomas boys; he's married to Jan Brown's oldest daughter." If someone did move away—for college or a job, maybe—they always seemed to navigate back home again. A retired couple might be "snowbirds" and head south to somewhere a bit warmer for two or three months in the winter, but they still called their small community home.

Unfortunately, that's not often the case today. People move frequently for work, and then choose to retire in different states. A 2008 Pew Social & Demographic Trends survey found nearly four in ten U.S.-born adults say the place they consider home isn't where they are living now, though I was heartened to see that the Midwest was the most "rooted" region, with nearly half of adults saying they have spent their whole lives in one community.

There's nothing wrong with feeling a little footloose, and it's terrific to see our young people travel and learn about other places as part of their education and life experience. However, there's a lot of good that comes from rootedness too. So many communities across Michigan and the rest of America are filled with people who have settled in for the long haul, and who fiercely protect their land, their neighbors and their community. Agricultural communities are remarkable in this regard. Their family, faith and livelihood are intertwined not only in how they live personally, but also in their generosity to their community.

Communities like Midland are filled with friends and neighbors who can guide us to play roles outside our own personal self-interest. They're our teachers and coaches, and our pastors and other religious leaders. They're members of the Scouts, 4H, athletic teams, the Rotary, Kiwanis Clubs and the American Legion Post. The list goes on.

Then there are corporations, directly and through their foundations and employees, that are often a tremendous source of community support. Habitat for Humanity of Michigan, for example, has benefited from contributions, goods and lots of hands-on support for team builds from such companies as Consumers Energy, The Dow Chemical Company, DTE Energy, Ford Motor Company, General Motors and Whirlpool Corporation. Many other companies similarly sponsor home builds in their communities and around the world.

These community leaders and organizations teach all of us, young and old alike. They reinforce basic values and help us work toward shared goals and commitments. Sometimes, they offer only the simple joy of belonging and contributing. Other times, they make remarkable and long-lasting contributions to society. But together, all of these parts work together to form that glorious whole we call "community."

I Knew You When

Both my family and Cynthia's family are fortunate to call Midland home. We take seriously the responsibility to look after—and fully appreciate the benefits we receive from—our hometown, including the friends and neighbors who live here. We consider ourselves fortunate that our children attended the same elementary, middle and high schools we did, an unusual event these days, and that the two of us first met as neighborhood kids.

Sometimes, however, that sense of community can feel pretty far away. My parents, sisters Sandra and Gretchen, and I moved to a new home in June 1959, and my father died that November. As mentioned, I was just six years old, and felt pretty alone in the world. Fortunately, I was surrounded by a family full of love and my mom and sisters and I helped and braced each other after our loss. Plus, we lived in a fun neighborhood. I also am grateful for the family next door with six kids, who welcomed me into their very lively home. We'd play army, football, basketball and capture the flag, or make rafts to float on the creek behind our houses. And there was always a chair ready to pull up to the dinner table for me to join them.

One of the children in the home next door was just a year older, and we became very good friends. His name was Dave Camp. I was Dave's campaign manager when he ran for student council president at Jefferson Intermediate School; the next year I was elected to the same position. Twenty-five years later, Dave was the one elected to succeed me in Congress. During his 24 years in national office, Dave was an exceptional congressman for our district and our country, and held critically important roles, including Chair of the Ways and Means Committee. I left my seat in the House to the friend who'd always left me a seat at his family's dinner table. How many members of Congress can say that?

The three amigos on a ski vacation in Utah in 1989 (l to r): me, Dave Camp and Tom Ludington. (Photo credit: Tom Ludington)

The third amigo growing up was Tom Ludington, whom I first met as an opponent on sports teams back in elementary and middle school. When his family moved to a new neighborhood, he was "forced" to attend the rival high school, which we still joke about. We were early rivals in school sports, but we've been on the same metaphorical team for decades now. U.S. Federal District Judge Tom Ludington has been on the bench since 2006. I am honored that he has sworn me in twice as Attorney General at the state Capitol in Lansing, most recently on a very chilly January 1, 2015. Tom also is a member of the Board of Trustees of the Rollin M. Gerstacker Foundation, where he serves with distinction just as he does on the bench as a judge.

I can remember when Tom, Dave and I were in our 20s, standing on a downtown rooftop back in 1981 or 1982. We looked out over "our town," boldly describing—as only young people can—how we would make Midland better, just as I hope young people all across our state and nation are also doing. The wonderful thing is that each of us went on to do something about improving our community, our state and our country.

Tom, Dave, and I were all in each other's weddings. We all went to law school, at one point we all practiced in Midland (though at different firms), and all of us have made our careers in public service. And we all still call the Midland area home.

Crisis and Community

Even if individuals today have become more mobile and less connected to each other, there are still those transcendent moments where we all draw closer as a community. The media likes to emphasize the controversies and differences among us, but in times of trouble we see and appreciate the good in all people. We witness communities banding together to support a cause or help others in need.

The September 11, 2001 attacks, for instance, will forever be etched in our national memory. But so will be our response to those attacks. I had stopped by to see Alan Ott after a doctor's appointment and before heading to Lansing, when we heard the news. A Korean War veteran and man of few but important words, he listened to the news reports and said quietly, "We're at war now."

The entire country drew together as one unified community. Local Red Cross chapters deployed volunteers, and students collected donations. Around the country, people who had never met each other supported those who suffered personal tragedy. As Gerald Ford said in Grand Rapids just a few days after the attacks, "This week, all Americans are neighbors. All of us are New Yorkers. All of us are Washingtonians. Most important, all of us are patriots."

According to a survey conducted by Indiana University's Center on Philanthropy two months after the 9/11 attacks, nearly 75 percent of American adults contributed in some way in the weeks following the terrorist attacks. We demonstrated to each other and the world that we are one united community of Americans.

On a less well-known, but still significant scale, after the devastating earthquake in Haiti in early 2010, Michigan farmers donated more than 500,000 eggs to feed victims. The donation was part of the national Good Egg Project, which contributed more than three million eggs to Feed the Children's Haitian relief efforts. The shells were cracked open and the liquid contents dried, then the product was flown to Haiti along with enough clean water to reconstitute the eggs. With typical humility, one of the farmers joked, "Even though they are my competition, [these fellow farmers] are good people."

Our challenge is to capture that sentiment during the daily grind, without requiring a natural disaster or other tragedy to generate that sense of unity. There are many organizations that help support and enhance our communities. Pick one or two that matter and get involved in your community.

Political Community — an Oxymoron?

Revitalizing our sense of togetherness is especially needed in the most fractured American community there is—one so acrimonious, in fact, that it seldom is considered much of a community these days. I'm referring, as you might have guessed, to our political system.

Much has been written and said about the divisiveness in politics today, and unfortunately, a lot of it is true. Red-faced pundits shouting at each other on cable TV. Politicians driving wedges instead of building consensus. A zero-sum mindset that encourages winning at all costs, even if that means the country loses.

It can all be pretty disheartening. But what we need to remember, whether the competition is sports, business or politics, is that adversaries do not have to be enemies.

When I came to Washington as a freshman congressman, the legendary Tip O'Neill was Speaker of the House. Another freshman congressman declared he would never shake Tip's hand because he so vehemently disagreed with the Speaker's viewpoints. Although I never was so rude as to shun the Speaker, I essentially followed the same path which, looking back, was just stupid and immature.

More seasoned and insightful politicians understand that whatever our differences, we are bound together by our shared desire to do great things on behalf of the American people. When he was president, Gerald Ford, for example, had a contentious political relationship with O'Neill, but the two were good personal friends while in office and long afterwards.

Standing in front of the Joe Louis statue at Cobo Hall in Detroit during a 1989 Republican State Convention (l to r): John Engler, Peter Secchia, L. Brooks Patterson and me. (Photo credit: Bill Schuette)

Ambassador Peter F. Secchia of Grand Rapids (though his wife Joan grew up in Midland and they were married here, as well), told me the story of seeing this friendship and broader perspective firsthand when he was a guest of then-President and Mrs. Ford at the White House. As he had coffee and read the *Washington Post* one morning, he was angered by a particularly critical quote about the President from Speaker O'Neill. When Ford walked into the room a short time later, Peter not only shared his irritation, but also suggested the president likewise respond to the unwarranted attack. As Peter recalls, the president grinned and said sometimes things had to be said publicly, but that he couldn't take the comments personally or out of the broader context. Ford played golf with his friend Tip later that afternoon, and reportedly had a candid and productive discussion. Later, Peter asked how he could golf with Tip after such criticism, Ford calmly replied, "You can disagree without being disagreeable."

Tip O'Neill's similarly friendly relationship with then-President Reagan is hailed as a lost model of bipartisanship. In his memoir, *Man of the House*, Tip describes his first meeting with Reagan shortly after the November 1980 election. "I reminded him that I had always been on good terms with the Republican leadership and that despite our various disagreements in the House, we were always friends after six o'clock and on weekends. The president-elect seemed to like that formulation, and over the next six years he would often begin our telephone discussions by saying 'Hello, Tip, is it after six o'clock?'

"'Absolutely, Mr. President,' I would respond. Our watches must have been in sync, because even with our many intense political battles, we managed to maintain a pretty good friendship."

I saw the same sense of collegiality in 2012, when I attended a reception for the state attorneys general at the U.S. Supreme Court. After the reception, we were invited into the courtroom itself. We all took our seats on the mahogany benches, surrounded by marble columns and facing the iconic nine chairs, one for each justice, elevated at the front of the room. The speaker that year was Associate Justice Elena Kagan, who had been appointed by President Obama in 2010. Justice Kagan has an impressive background, including serving as Dean of Harvard Law School and as U.S. Solicitor General.

Still, given our respective political leanings, I figured we wouldn't have much in common and was prepared to disagree with what I would see and hear. You can imagine my surprise, when Justice Kagan walked in from the back of the room rather than the front, smiled warmly at all of us and said, "Hi." I was immediately impressed by her informal approach— such a pleasant contrast to the intimidating setting and, quite frankly, to my expectations. I was even more surprised when, midway through her remarks, she called out, "Michigan." I raised my hand from the back of the room where I was sitting and Justice Kagan continued, "Your solicitor general is incredible. He wears those bow ties, but when he speaks, he commands the attention of the entire courtroom."

She was right. Former Michigan Solicitor General John Bursch is an exceptional attorney, and Michigan was very fortunate to benefit from his talent. I agreed with and thanked her, then sat back, stunned. I thought it was incredibly gracious of her to so publicly compliment John. And it was incredibly ungracious of me to assume I wouldn't appreciate Justice Kagan. I thanked her again personally after the talk, and sent her a follow-up thank-you note when I returned home, which she responded to, as well. I was reminded that while I may not always agree with her, Justice Kagan is not only highly intelligent, but also courteous and pleasant. I'm thankful for our continued collegial relationship.

It was yet another lesson that when we share common values, whether it's in politics, law or any other community, we can enjoy each other personally and work together professionally even when we disagree on specific policies. And it was yet another lesson about not prejudging others.

Tear Down Those Walls

In the end, I've learned that community at its most fundamental level is defined by common values. This was driven home for me in one remarkable moment.

As the Berlin Wall was being torn down in late 1989, the chaos was remarkable. People on both sides—East and West—were working passionately to bring down the wall. I visited Berlin during this historic event and through the U.S. Embassy, I had the opportunity to meet with some of the freedom fighters at a nearby café. I asked them why they would risk their lives—and their families' lives—for this. And I remember the immediate and direct response like it was yesterday: "Because people want to be free."

That compelling drive for freedom has brought together communities throughout history. In this case, Eastern and Western Germans were united as one. It's a reminder that people everywhere, across lines of division, are part of the same community of human beings. As then-President John F. Kennedy put it decades before that Wall was torn down, "For, in the final analysis, our most basic common link is that we all inhabit this small planet. We all breathe the same air. We all cherish our children's futures. And we are all mortal."

In these divisive days, we'd do well to remember the fundamental values that bind us together. We need to go the extra mile and be there for one another. Whether we're talking about Berlin, Germany, or the township of Berlin, Michigan, we need to tear down more walls—and maybe even build more Tridges.

You Don't Write the Script

"Faith is taking the first step even when you don't see the whole staircase."

—Martin Luther King, Jr.

The Road to Midland

When Paul the Apostle experienced his epiphany, it was accompanied by a flash of light and heavenly voices, blinding him for three days. Now, US-10 into Midland isn't exactly the road to Damascus, but in the summer of 1990 I had an epiphany of my own.

Her name was Cynthia.

At that point, Cynthia and I had only been dating for about a month, but our relationship had already become very serious. We had the same values, similar hopes and dreams for our lives, and were realizing we wanted to go there together —something we had apparently missed all those mornings on the bus to junior high. So I was intrigued one Sunday afternoon in July, right before the U.S. Senate primary, when Cynthia called and said she wanted to talk with me. I said "sure" and waited for her to arrive, knowing Sunday was her only day off from work, and I was days away from a competitive primary for the Senate.

When she showed up, Cynthia told me that as our relationship grew, she also wanted that to include our faith relationship. She needed to know that I believed Jesus Christ was my savior and that I was committed to a strong, personal faith. We talked and prayed that afternoon. It was a pivotal moment for us, but also for me personally. It helped me understand, even in the midst of a difficult campaign, that I needed and wanted to further develop my faith.

Growing up, our family went to church on Sundays, but I was not particularly active religiously as a child or young adult. My personal faith evolved over time and like so many important milestones in my life, it happened with Cynthia's support and encouragement. The way I think about it, I started out with a two-legged stool, supported by my career and family. Cynthia helped me with those two and just as importantly, with the third and stabilizing leg of faith.

As many of us have experienced, faith often flows from adversity. After my 1990 Senate loss—just a few months after Cynthia and I had our conversation—I spent a lot of time reflecting on what had happened and what it meant. Having planned my political path for so long, I felt pretty lost now that it had all come crashing down. I was confused and adrift. But ultimately, I came to see the light. And while I took tactical and political lessons from my defeat, the most meaningful lesson I learned was to accept that I am not in charge. There is One who designs the journey, and I am not the designer.

Faith and Friendship

As a young congressman in the U.S House of Representatives during the late 1980s, I avoided the weekly House Breakfast Group. I thought it was mostly just Bible study, and didn't see the point when there were so many other priorities on my calendar. In reality, this informal, bipartisan, interfaith group was intended to build personal relationships and break down barriers away from the House floor or committee rooms. It was open to all House members; there was a similar group in the Senate. The meetings began with a Scripture reading, followed by a member talking about their background and anything they wanted to share about themselves.

On several occasions, G.V. "Sonny" Montgomery, a Mississippi Democrat in the U.S. House of Representatives and senior statesman, invited me to attend. He'd pat me on the back and say, "Son, you ought to come to the House Breakfast Group. You'd like it, Bill." While I appreciated Sonny's kindness in personally inviting me, I still never went. Thinking back on it now, I realize he was reaching out not only to a colleague, but to a young guy who would have benefited from this broader perspective. I wish now that I had gone.

I remembered those invitations when I was out of the House and back in Michigan, serving in the state Senate. The organizers from D.C. encouraged me to think about a similar group in Michigan. After some particularly long sessions and late nights, I decided that the same collegial gatherings

To Bill & Cynthia,
Best Wishes

President George W. Bush, an old friend, at a dinner Cynthia and I attended in July 2004. (Photo credit: Reflections Photography/Washington, D.C.)

could be helpful in Lansing too. So I approached State Sen. Gary Peters (now a U.S. senator), a Democrat I enjoyed and respected despite—and perhaps because of—how often we sparred over legislation. Gary and I were like the coyote and sheepdog on the old Bugs Bunny cartoons who fought at work, but then walked off the set, punched their time cards at the end of the day, smiled and said, "See you tomorrow."

Gary agreed to help launch the Michigan Senate Breakfast Group meetings, which we scheduled monthly. We followed the same format used in Congress in Washington, D.C.: a Scripture reading at the beginning, breakfast, a senator sharing his or her story, and a closing prayer. The purpose was the same, as well—to build relationships and break down barriers between parties. State Rep. John Moolenaar (now a U.S. representative), started a similar program in the Michigan House, and both groups continue to meet. At a time when many Americans have lost touch with their faith, I believe these types of groups and programs provide a much-needed foundation for the values and lessons we have been taught, and which bind us together.

Public Service, Private Faith

For people in public life, balancing our faith with our public role can be difficult. There are some who feel compelled that their religion determines their votes. Others might consider their constituents to be the highest authority. There are those who feel comfortable speaking about their faith in public venues, and others who are not. I tend to be in the latter camp.

One day, in the midst of my tough primary race for the U.S. Senate, George W. and Laura Bush were in Detroit for a campaign event at a Tigers baseball game. My Republican opponent, Clark Durant, had a strong evangelical following and was highlighting his faith in the campaign. During a quiet moment together, I asked the Bush's what they thought about such a public display and discussion of faith in political campaigns. They told me that they believed that faith and public service are not incompatible, and that it was appropriate in the public discourse. I was surprised by that, yet as I listened to them and thought about it afterward, what they said made sense. You don't have to be ostentatious about it, but public service certainly goes hand-in-hand with public faith.

Still, while I'm a person with a strong faith and try to follow the Bible's lessons in both my personal and professional life, I don't wear it on my sleeve at public events. Instead I begin each day with a Bible reading and some personal reflection, and strive to make my words and actions—as well as the example I set at home, in the workplace, and with my constituents—consistent with Scripture.

I return often to the words in the Bible of Proverbs 2, which I quoted in my inaugural remarks after being sworn in as Attorney General in 2011: "Incline your ear to wisdom, And apply your heart to understanding." For me, it's a constant reminder to listen carefully and be thoughtful. After all, our constituents have placed a faith of their own in their elected leaders, and it's up to us to uphold it.

You Don't Write the Script

Those of us who have been entrusted with positions of leadership hold a lot of responsibility in our hands. And it's our task to make our corner of the world a better place. But we also need to have the humility to recognize that it's not all up to us. As John Quincy Adams is said to have declared, "Duty is ours; results are God's."

Now, I can tell you that no politician wants to take the stage professing powerlessness. Of course we all want to believe that our future is in our hands, and that our destiny is of our own making. But as I've learned through hard experience, we don't always get to write the script. That doesn't mean you should throw up your hands and do nothing. What it does mean is that you must have faith. Faith not just in your own talents and abilities, but faith in a higher power and that the writer of the journey is not you.

Our daughter Heidi was having trouble breathing immediately following her birth and Cynthia had not even had a chance to hold her new daughter. I was beside myself and said, "Give that baby back to her mother." The nurse, sensing the emotion of a new father, silently handed Heidi to Cynthia, who began singing "Jesus Loves Me, This I Know" to her, just as she had done throughout the pregnancy. Heidi's breathing returned to normal. I had no doubt about His presence with us.

Even in our own families, there's only so much we can control. Our children will have their own faith journeys, and all we can do is hope that we've helped them find their own belief in God and identify the importance of religious belief in their lives.

When people ask about my future career goals, the big difference from my early political days is that I don't know where the path leads, and I'm fine not knowing. What I do know is that there's a higher power out there who will guide our way. We must still work hard and try to make good decisions, but we need to be focused on taking one day at a time and making sure our priorities—in my case, family, faith and career—remain balanced.

I'll stop writing now, but I know that He will continue writing my script.

Families Make Peanut Brittle

"Your success as a family, our success as a society, depends not on what happens inside the White House, but on what happens inside your house."

—Barbara Bush

Turn Off the Juice When Not in Use

The Irish playwright George Bernard Shaw once commented that "Perhaps the greatest social service that can be rendered by anybody to the country and to mankind is to bring up a family." Shaw wasn't exactly the greatest family man—having had no children but multiple affairs—but he was right on the money with that one.

Our families are our earliest role models, writing the initial script influencing how we see the world. We then test and challenge those beliefs, validating some and modifying others as we grow and write our own story. What's more, our families offer us comfort and support. They're our companions around the dinner table and on weekend outings. And when we're old enough to raise our own kids, family is what we build to ensure they grow up happy, healthy and loved.

My parents were high school sweethearts in Cleveland, Ohio, a couple of kids during the Depression with barely two nickels to rub together. Dad was quite an athlete and

Mom saved all the pictures and articles about him, which I love reading. Early on, they instilled their values in my sisters and me: Work hard, keep your promises, stay down-to-earth and live simply. One of my early memories of Dad is of him walking through the house, turning off lights and saying, "Turn off the juice when not in use." As a little kid, I was

The Schuette family in 1958 in our Midland backyard (l to r): sister Gretchen, mother Esther, sister Sandra, me and father Bill. (Photo credit : Schuette family)

pretty confused about what apple juice had to do with turning off the lights.

Dad's rise through The Dow Chemical Company was largely based on and certainly consistent with these values. When he died at age 47, we suddenly found ourselves a single-parent family. My mom did her best to make sure my two sisters, Sandra and Gretchen, and I were raised with love and as normal a family life as possible under the circumstances. It couldn't have been easy, but I don't remember her ever complaining. I do remember Sandra and Gretchen stepping in to help their little brother, though, fielding baseballs or rebounding basketballs on the driveway or helping me with my homework.

My mother was the best campaigner in the family. She met then-presidential candidate George H.W. Bush at the MBS (Midland, Bay, Saginaw) airport proudly wearing this homemade sign around her neck. (Credit: Bill Schuette)

Mom was always my biggest cheerleader, and probably the best politician in the family. She just loved the political stuff. When I first worked for George H.W. Bush in 1980, we flew into Tri-City Airport for some rally. And there was mom, meeting the president with a sign around her neck that said, "I am Bill Schuette's mother." That was vintage mom, always looking out for me.

I also found familial solace in other places. My hero back then was Chip Hilton, a fictional character in a book series that I loved as a young boy. The Chip character also had lost his father at a young age too, so I could readily relate to the books. Clair Bee, a former Long Island University basketball coach, was the author of 24 Chip Hilton books, and I read every one as soon as I could get my hands on them.

Chip was a three-sport athlete—football quarterback, basketball forward and baseball pitcher. Chip's team often won, but everything didn't work out until the very end of the book, for gosh sakes (as Chip would say). The small-town values of Bee's hometown in West Virginia, just 10 miles from the setting for the early books, echoed Midland's.

In those books I found, in some respects, a surrogate brother—at least on paper. With Dad gone, it was hard to be a chip off the old block. But I could try to be a chip off Chip.

And by the way, I still have that set of books. When our son was young, he would play outside or engage in any athletic activity you could name, but had zero interest in reading. Cynthia and I did not know what to do to kindle his interest in reading. One day, I thought about the Chip Hilton stories and we had him read *Freshman Quarterback*. A reading fire was ignited and to this day Bill is an all-consuming, voracious reader.

As I grew, I learned more about my father through stories told about him, some of which could have rivaled Chip's own. His larger-than-life legacy—of being smart and highly respected while also remaining personable and down-to-earth—was etched into me, even though I didn't have much time to know him myself. Trying to measure up to him and his reputation was intimidating. But even years after his passing, the values and foundation my father set at home, at work and in the community guided me. I knew I wouldn't be able to go toe-to-toe with him in business, so consciously or subconsciously, I looked for a different way to succeed. I think that was my initial motivation for getting into politics. I hoped I could be equally successful, and that it would have made my father proud. To this day, he remains my inspiration; when I leave a room I often can hear his voice reminding me to turn off the lights.

Politics and Family Life — Like Oil and Water?

Whenever a politician resigns under a cloud of scandal, the time-honored claim is that he or she is leaving office "to spend more time with family." The euphemism may be deceptive, but it does hint at a broader truth: It's hard to hold a high-powered position and still make time for family. Certainly for me, this is probably the hardest issue to manage.

Politics can take a heavy toll on families. Like so many professions, there is the constant push and pull of priorities, with evening meetings, travel and inevitable scheduling conflicts. In Congress, families are either back at home with the member of Congress flying back and forth on weekends, or the family moves to the D.C. area, often uprooting kids from their friends and spouses from their work. Nobody wants to have to choose between a child's soccer game or ballet recital and a critical vote on a bill, but sometimes familial duties run smack up against governing ones.

The strain of campaigning can also be tough, especially after a major loss. In the best-case scenarios, candidates pursue related or new careers and the family resumes a normal life. In the worst of cases, candidates struggle to cope and can turn to alcohol or other vices, driving a downward spiral in their professional careers and personal lives. Sadly, the high price of a political career has destroyed more than one marriage.

Cynthia and I started our family when I was Michigan's Director of Agriculture, and the challenge of traveling between Lansing and Midland was tough enough. During those early parenting days, I tried—unsuccessfully, I might add—to multi-task. Often, I would find myself changing a diaper at home while on the phone with someone in Lansing. And what would happen? The diaper would fall off a short time later, and I'm pretty sure the conversation fared no better. I learned then that I needed to focus on one thing at a time—just a few major priorities in a day—rather than trying to do everything, but doing nothing well. Balancing all those responsibilities was tough, however, and it remains a challenge for me today. It's a big part of the reason that I chose to continue my political career in Michigan, rather than add in the additional demands of traveling back and forth between Midland and D.C.

As much as politics can and do affect your family, the reverse is also true. Families change your political sensitivity and perspective as well.

One of the first votes I took in Congress was on a bill to establish Daylight Savings Time. As a 31-year-old single man, I was ambivalent. My staff described for me young children standing in single-digit temperatures at pitch-black bus stops, and our office received calls and letters from constituents. I saw the logic and voted for it. But it wasn't until later, when I was the parent of school-age children myself, that I fully appreciated those passionate letters and calls from parents. A few years later, I also voted to reauthorize the Civil Rights Act and to establish the Martin Luther King holiday. My sister had adopted two mixed-race children several years earlier and I had learned to see—through their eyes—the significance of these bills.

There's no question that we are guided and sometimes driven by events that occur in our families, as well as in our communities. These experiences provide perspective and passion that often push us from being a spectator in politics or life, to getting in the game and making a difference in our world.

In short, family responsibilities can be a challenge to navigate in politics. But our families very often help us understand and remember the reason for doing what we're doing in the first place.

The Unsung Heroes in a Politician's Family

While Mitt Romney didn't win the 2012 presidential election, *MITT*, the documentary following Romney on the campaign trail illustrated his family's commitment to the campaign. As the *Boston Globe* noted, "It shows him asking his family for guidance, leaning on them for laughter, or kneeling with them in prayer."

After a horrific car accident took the lives of Vice President Joe Biden's first wife and daughter and gravely injured his two sons, Biden's family stepped in. In his book, *Promises to Keep*, Biden says his sister Valerie and her husband Bruce moved in to help when the boys were released from the hospital. He notes they "never really talked about it, but the Biden family rule applied: If you have to ask for help, it's too late."

Tragically, one of those sons, Beau, died of brain cancer in May 2015. The Biden family has endured such incredible loss, but through it we also have seen such incredible love, faith and strength in their family.

It isn't always something as tragic as a death in the family. It can be as simple as pitching in when a family member is sick, or laid off or just overworked. But it all goes back to those small-town values. Your family helps in times of need.

I know mine certainly did. It was all hands on deck in the summer of 1984, during my first campaign. The staff had quit because of some internal organizational issues, but unfortunately it was right in the middle of the campaign. And without fanfare, my mom, Carl, Sandra and Gretchen stepped in. They became my campaign staff.

Each of my sisters took turns coming to Midland, with Sandra coming from Connecticut and Gretchen from Oregon. They brought their families with them, and each spent a full month working on the campaign. My stepfather took over managing everything, with the field representatives reporting directly to him. Mom recruited volunteers. That first race wasn't just a campaign; it ended up being a family event. My

My sisters (l to r): Gretchen and Sandra, who have loved and put up with me, their little brother, all their lives. (Photo credit: Gretchen Schuette)

family provided the gas when things were sputtering. I would not have won but for them.

But perhaps the most remarkable heroes—or, in my case, heroine—are the spouses of politicians. They rarely bask in the limelight or receive public recognition when they should, but they steadfastly keep the family together, making sure that meals magically appear and that homework gets done. When someone in the family is sick or something goes wrong, our spouses gamely pick up the pieces and fill in the gaps.

When I'm driving home from an evening event, with appreciative comments still ringing in my ears, I think about how they should really be thanking Cynthia. She made it possible. Whatever the event is, I couldn't have attended if she hadn't effectively taken on the role of both parents.

Make Some Peanut Brittle

Not long ago, Alan Ott pulled me aside for another piece of advice I needed to hear. "Bill," he said, "you need to go home and make some peanut brittle."

I was as stumped as you. "Okay, but what does that mean?" I asked.

So Al explained. While he loves peanut brittle, he is allergic to peanuts. But for Jean, his wife of almost 60 years, making the candy together is an important Christmas tradition in their family. And so, for more years than he can count, Al has happily and dutifully been home to make peanut brittle. Because it matters to her. Because most importantly, it's

Election night in 2010, just after Cynthia learned I had won the election to become Attorney General of Michigan. (Photo credit: Associated Press)

about going home and focusing on those you love and your relationship with them.

Message received, Mr. Ott.

Fast-forward to November 2014, shortly after the election results came in for Attorney General. I received a brief text from Jim Barrett, my campaign chair, who had heard me tell Al's story. His note was as kind as it was direct: "Go home and make some peanut brittle."

Family is a gift. From the early days of changing diapers, to getting our children through drivers' education to watching them leave home for college—the role of parents can be pretty humbling and certainly keeps you grounded.

Jean and Alan Ott, wonderful friends and mentors of the Schuette family and so many others in the Midland area. (Photo credit: Rollin M. Gerstacker Foundation)

Cynthia's father Carl Grebe, my mother Esther Schuette Gerstacker,
and me in 1992. (Photo credit: Bill Schuette)

Our children are now young adults, but I look at them
sometimes when they come home to visit, and still see the
young children they once were. I have to remind myself—
and they often take the opportunity to remind me—that
they're growing up. Although my parents have passed away, I
see the special father-daughter relationship Cynthia has with
her 96-year-old father (a veteran WWII fighter pilot). The
advice and support we provide one another may change over
time, but the love doesn't. As Barbara Bush once said, "To
us, family means putting your arms around each other and
being there."

It's not always easy. And sometimes you've got to make
sure you go home and make a little peanut brittle to keep

the family connected and chugging along. But coming from a place where family is what fuels me, I've learned that no matter how busy you are, whatever you're doing won't mean much if you don't invest first in being a good parent, spouse or caring sibling. The rest is all significant, but family is the foundation that makes it all worthwhile.

CONCLUSION

When You're Ready To Serve, You're Ready To Lead

Small-town America has much to teach us, as I've tried to show in this book. Like my hometown of Midland, small communities really are just a microcosm of big cities and regions. Even if you live in a big city, these small town values can run deep in your neighborhood, your community associations, and are vibrant in your synagogue or house of worship. The difference is that small towns like mine are a place where you can experience, up close, the values and leadership that shape our lives. You can watch and participate with individuals and organizations that work together— sometimes over decades— to drive long-term improvements for their families, friends and neighbors. Our communities teach us valuable, lifelong lessons about dedication to hard work, about humility and about resilience. They are filled with people who show us, often by quiet example, what it really means to be committed to and supported by family, faith and community.

These hometown values show us how to serve others. Because people in small towns know each other so well, they understand and can incorporate the needs of others in their community. We have to rely on each other; it's the only way to get things done, even when or especially when, there are differences of opinion. No one person or organization can make major changes alone.

For me, it is always inspiring to see the remarkable results that come from working together, from blending our agendas, pooling our talents and joining our strengths. That is one of the many lessons I have learned over the years from the leaders with whom I've had the good fortune to work, starting with my earliest friends, family and mentors, and continuing through to the work I am privileged to do every day.

When I lost sight of some of these lessons early in my professional life, I had to get back up, dust myself off and return to those hometown values that are the most important, both personally and professionally. In the years since, those values have been my foundation. They ground me, as do my family and my faith, in what matters the most. They inspire me to continue to grow and contribute.

The biggest lesson I've tried to hang onto is to remain absolutely focused on and committed to service. When we stay fully focused on the people we're aiming to serve, rather than on ourselves, we listen better, learn more and are able to do more good in the world. We become, in short, better leaders.

It's only when we're truly dedicated to service that we're also ready to lead.

INDEX

A

B

D

E

F

G

S